Mary—The Feminine Face of the Church

BELLA MATRIBUS DESTESTATA

(War, which all mothers hate)

Mary—
The Feminine Face of the Church

by
ROSEMARY RADFORD RUETHER

THE WESTMINSTER PRESS

Philadelphia

Book Design by Dorothy Alden Smith

Published by The Westminster Press ®
Philadelphia, Pennsylvania
PRINTED IN THE UNITED STATES OF AMERICA

9 8 7 6 5 4 3 2

Library of Congress Cataloging in Publication Data

Ruether, Rosemary Radford.
 Mary, the feminine face of the Church.

 1. Mary, Virgin. I. Title.
BT602.R83   232.91   77–7652
ISBN   0–664–24759–8

CONTENTS

Preface

Some books are published and marketed with the intention that they will long grace tabletops in comfortable living rooms. This book was never intended for so glamorous a future. It is being published with the intention that it will serve as a well-worn text for the women and men of today's church who find themselves reconsidering the traditional doctrines, practices, and teachings of the church.

Long before the feminist movement, Mary, the mother of Jesus, and to a lesser extent the sisters Mary and Martha were used as standard references on occasions that required consideration of women within the church. Even on such occasions these Biblical women were portrayed as auxiliary persons, however dignified the "helper" status might have been. Especially within the Reformed tradition, Christians have viewed Mary in a subordinate role. Many Protestants view Mary largely through their somewhat distorted perception of Mariology within Roman Catholicism. For many Protestants the dogma of the Roman Catholic Church in relation to Mary has been mysterious and inscrutable.

The present work makes a significant contribution to our understanding of Mariology as a vital doctrine for the contemporary church. For Protestants the chapter entitled "Mary and the Protestants" enlightens a history which had long since become murky. Rosemary Ruether in this volume, as in so many others, has aided us in grappling with our religious heritage, Scriptural authority, and contemporary culture. Through her careful Biblical scholarship she enables us to reclaim a part of our religious tradition that has so long been ignored.

This volume originally appeared as a series of articles in *Enquiry: Bible Studies for the Laity,* Vol. 9, No. 2 (December 1976–February 1977), published by The Geneva Press. Because of the importance and excellence of the work, it has been published as a separate volume so that it can become a lasting part of our libraries on Biblical studies. For beyond helping us to reclaim tradition and apprehend Scripture, this work gives us a glimpse of the truly feminine face of the church.

UNITED PRESBYTERIAN WOMEN,
National Executive Committee,
The United Presbyterian Church U.S.A.

Part I

MARY IN THE BIBLE

INTRODUCTION

It is popularly assumed among Protestants that traditional doctrines about Mary, the mother of Jesus, are a false development within Roman Catholicism and do not have a Biblical foundation. To Protestants, even doctrines such as that of the virgin birth are primarily teaching about Jesus Christ. To make Mary herself a separate source of piety for Christians is thought to be wrong.

However, the contemporary women's movement in the churches has raised some new questions. Is Protestantism too masculine? Why are all its religious symbols male? We speak of Father and of Son and of brethren, but never of Mother, daughter, or sisters. Is there any basis for feminine symbols in Christianity? How can women find a place in the church? These questions have caused some Protestant women to look at teachings about Mary with new eyes. Maybe there are some positive elements for Protestants in Mary, who is so esteemed by other branches of the church.

Contemporary feminists are not the first to feel that there is something "unbalanced" in an all-male religious language. A generation ago the eminent theologian Paul Tillich suggested that Protestantism was too male-oriented. It needed some of the feminine element provided through Mary in Roman Catholicism. Tillich even said that his view of God as the "ground of being" was more a "mothering" symbol than a "fathering" symbol.

Yet, paradoxically, those churches which esteem Mary are not especially open to women. Catholicism and Eastern Orthodoxy forbid the ministry to women. They seem to assign a passive role to women in the laity as well.

How, then, is the veneration of Mary related to Biblical religion? Is Mary a liberator for women, or is she more a tool of male power over women? Are there important ideas here that Protestantism has overlooked?

1
MARY
AND THE ANCIENT GODDESS

I Kings, ch. 18; Acts 19:21–41

It is often said that Mary is a survival of the goddess figures of ancient Near Eastern religion. Such statements are often taken to discredit teaching about Mary as a true part of Christian teaching. But many Biblical symbols, festivals, and institutions also were common to the ancient Near Eastern cultures. For example, the idea of the Messiah had its roots in the age-old concept of the God-King. (See Ps. 2 and 110.) The king in those societies was understood as a representative of the gods to the human world, and also a representative of society before the gods. He was a savior. Upon his justice and righteousness depended the welfare of the people. Many insights arose among others and were taken over by writers of Biblical religion. We need to examine such ideas on their own merits.

The Goddess as a Symbol of Life

In the earliest cultures unearthed by archaeologists, figures of mother goddesses have been found. These small statues depict full-breasted, pregnant women. They come from pre-agricultural hunting societies. They are generally found without accompanying male symbols for the gods.

In this period the human community was surrounded by nature. Nature itself gave or withheld life. People hunted and gathered, but they did not control the forces of life. They did

13

not plant or irrigate. Women gave birth according to mysterious powers that were not understood. As birth giver, woman became the symbol for all the forces of life.

In many myths of these ancient peoples there was talk about the birth of the world from a "world egg." There was no "god" outside the "egg" who created the world from above. Rather, the "world egg" was like a womb that fertilized itself and gave birth to heaven and earth, gods and humans.

The mother as goddess was even spoken of as the "mother of gods and men." Pairs of heavenly gods, male and female, were believed to have been born out of this womb or matrix. The modern idea of God as "ground of being" has preserved this ancient idea of god as a matrix or womb out of which all of life arose.

The Goddess as Virgin and Mother

Out of the world egg came several generations of gods. First there was the sky-father and the earth-mother; then there were their children, who represented the various life-forces of sky and earth. The god-king was usually associated with one of these younger gods. He was not the original creator, but was the son of the sky-father and the earth-mother. He was associated with a goddess who was at the same time his mother, wife, and sister.

This kind of thinking was found in the new urban societies founded in the Eastern Mediterranean from 4000 to 2000 B.C., which was long before Abraham. The human king was allied with the mother goddess to create the harmonious ordering of the forces of life and nature.

The mother goddess and the king played the central roles in public worship, originally on New Year's Day. The New Year ceremony depicted in song, story, and drama the rebirth of nature after the summer-fall drought. Every year in summer the vegetation was overcome by the power of death. The god-king, who represented vegetation, was believed to sink

14

down into the underworld. It was the mother goddess who defeated the power of death. She gathered together the scattered pieces of the god-king's body. She resurrected him from the dead. He then took his throne in a renewed world.

This rebirth of the god-king was climaxed by the sacred marriage. After the marriage of the reborn king and the goddess, the new child, the new lamb, and the new grain of the new year were born. The king was both the spouse and the son of the goddess. He reigned over the universe from her lap. In Egyptian tradition, the mother goddess Isis was even called the "throne." Traditional Christian pictures of Jesus as a baby king with the world in one hand and a scepter in the other, reigning from the lap of the Virgin Mary, had their origin in this traditional picture of the Egyptian mother goddess Isis and the new god-king, Horus.

The mother goddess was not a passive figure. She was an active agent in the drama of the renewal of life. In some sense she was the encompassing power which determined that life dies and is reborn again. From her lap the king reigned over the world. She was seen as a mighty warrior. She was both virgin and mother. Although ever fertile, she never grew old. She was always innocent and fresh. She was never the possession of anyone. She always preserved her independence and autonomy. She stamped her foot and shook the throne of heaven.

Prayer of Lamentation
to Ishtar (Babylonian Mother Goddess)

I pray to thee, O Lady of ladies,
  goddess of goddesses,
O Ishtar, queen of all peoples, who
  guides mankind aright.
. . . .
O supporter of arms, who determines battle,
O possessor of all divine power, who
  wears the crown of dominion,

O Lady, glorious is thy greatness; over
    all the gods it is exalted.

. . . .

The judgment of the people in truth and
    righteousness thou indeed dost decide.
Thou regardest the oppressed and mistreated;
    daily thou causest them to prosper.
Thy mercy! O Lady of heaven and earth,
    shepherdess of the weary people.

. . . .

Where thou dost look, one who is dead
    lives; one who is sick rises up;
The erring one who sees thy face goes
    aright.
I have cried to thee, suffering, wearied,
    and distressed, as thy servant.
See me, O my Lady; accept my prayers.
Faithfully look upon me and hear my
    supplication.
Promise my forgiveness and let thy spirit
    be appeased.

> *—From "Prayer of Lamentation to
> Ishtar," tr. by Ferris J. Stephens, in*
> Ancient Near Eastern Texts
> Relating to the Old Testament,
> *2d ed., ed. by James B. Pritchard
> (Princeton University Press, 1950,
> 1955)*

The Goddess as Virgin, Not Mother

In the mythology of classical Greece one finds a further
development of the image of the goddess. Each aspect of the
great mother goddess of the Near East was depicted as a
separate female figure. There was Artemis the huntress (see
Acts, ch. 19); Athena, the warrior maiden; Aphrodite, the
love goddess; and Hera, the mother-wife. But there was also
a distinct hostility to the goddess as wife and mother. Hera,

the wife of Zeus, for example, was reduced to a nagging, petulant figure.

The most dignified female figures in Greek mythology were virgins. In them the maiden had been separated from sexuality and motherhood. This was particularly true of Athena, the patroness of Athens. She scorned marriage and knew nothing of motherhood. She was snatched from the blasted womb of her mother, to be born from the head of her father, Zeus. She was the companion of warriors, the inspirer of heroism in men. She was even made the advocate of the growing power of men over women.

So, then, it seems that in Greek mythology we can see a tendency to block out the ancient symbols of the woman as mother. Sexuality and maternity were considered inferior powers. The female symbol was split into a lower biological force and a higher spiritual force. Only the goddess as virgin could cooperate in the higher works of men.

In the classical period of ancient Greek society we know that the wife was assigned a very inferior position. She was confined to the back of the house. She took no part in public society. The woman as wife and mother was not thought to be a fit spiritual companion of the male. Only men or a few exceptional unmarried women could really enter into the higher friendship of the spirit. Greek thought is very important for understanding the fear of the body, of sexuality, and of women that began to shape classical society and that greatly influenced Christianity.

The Goddess and Life After Death

Our sketch of the goddess in antiquity would not be complete without mentioning a final stage of development close to the time of the rise of Christianity. Under Rome the ancient nature religions, once centered in the goddess and the king, had lost their political basis. The rites of rebirth of the old nature religions were converted into mystery religions of life after death. These religions became traveling missionary religions. The rebirth they offered was now the personal re-birth of the soul to life after death, rather than the rebirth of the earth and society from the forces of drought, famine, and conquest.

The religion of Isis, the Egyptian goddess, was one proto-type of many of the ideas taken over in Christian teaching about Mary. Chastity typified her image and worship. Her priests were tonsured and celibate. Fasting, prayer, vigils, and moral renewal preceded the initiation of her devotees. She appeared as a beautiful figure who rose from the sea, crowned with the moon, wearing a dark mantle bordered with stars. On the basis of moral renewal of their lives, her devotees were promised prosperity in this life and assurance of life after death. She was above all wisdom, the companion of purified souls. When the religion of Isis was defeated by Christianity, much of her power and attraction lived on in the devotion to Mary.

For Thought and Discussion

Our images of God are drawn from human experience.

1. Let the members of the group list those attributes which they associate with the idea of father. Then list those they associate with the idea of mother. What differences seem to emerge? Why?

2. Now try to visualize God as mother. What different characteristics would seem to emerge from thinking of God as mother? How is this image different from thinking of God as father? Does God as Father in the Biblical tradition also have "mothering" qualities? Is something lost in our image of God when we think of God only as Father? Discuss.

2
MARY AND ISRAEL—GOD'S BRIDE

Hosea, chs. 1 to 3; The Song of Solomon

Old Testament religion is traditionally presented to us as an uncompromising war against nature religion. The worship of Yahweh (the LORD in English translations of the Old Testament) totally rejected that religion of Canaan expressed by the worship of the god-king Baal and the goddess Anath. This struggle between Yahwism and the religion of Canaan was one of the most important influences in shaping Old Testament religion. The Old Testament rejection of female symbols for God, and perhaps also of female religious leaders, probably had something to do with this struggle against Canaanite religion, with its powerful goddess figures and its female-dominated ceremonies of worship.

It is too simple, however, to see Yahweh as the God of history who rejects the gods of nature. Current views of the Old Testament reflect our modern divorce from agricultural society and from the world of nature. In the Old Testament there is no divorce between history and nature. Rather, the two were interconnected in God's covenant with Israel.

When people were unfaithful to God, both society and nature fell into chaos. (See, for example, Isa., ch. 24.) Thus God's wrath at the unfaithfulness of the people was expressed both in historical misfortunes, such as conquests by foreign powers, and in blight and drought upon the land. God was a God who gave and withheld rain and fertility on the earth. The seasons of excessive drought and famine expressed divine

19

displeasure and caused the human community to search itself for its sins.

The Land Prospers

When Israel is faithful to God and there is justice and harmony in society, there follows abundant fertility and blessedness in the land. The concept of the land is a very important idea in the Old Testament. It is the central gift of God to Israel. Its being given and its being taken away, its fertility and its barrenness, are a kind of thermometer that can measure the relationship between God and Israel.

All the language of the old fertility religion was transformed to express the death and rebirth of the land. Now it expressed the moral relationship of God and Israel. The land withered and died when Israel and God were alienated from each other. The land flowered in abundant prosperity, ran with life-giving waters, and overflowed with milk and honey when God and Israel were reconciled. The old language of nature was taken over in the Psalms and the Prophets to express the alienation or reconciliation of Israel with God. (Compare Amos 4:6–13 and ch. 9:13–15.)

Israel believed that Canaan was the land promised by God to his people. Yet the Old Testament also tells us that this land was taken by Israel through invasion and conquest of the non-Hebrew people who lived there. In ancient times the conquest of a people was also thought to mean the conquest of their gods. The conquering people proved through the fact of conquest the superiority and greater might of their gods and the inferiority of the gods of the conquered people. Israel added to this rather crude idea of a god of superior might the belief that its God also commanded superior righteousness. Israel particularly rejected the sexual practice of religious prostitution associated with the religions of fertility. The Canaanite worship of Baal and Anath was summed up in one Old Testament word: harlotry. To worship the old Canaanite gods was to "play the harlot," like an unfaithful wife who sought other lovers. (See Hos., ch. 2.)

Queen of Heaven

We know that this struggle to supplant the gods of Canaan with the worship of Yahweh was not immediately successful. The non-Israelite people among whom Israel lived continued to practice the old religion. Many Israelites intermarried with these people and adopted some of their practices. Jeremiah tells us that in time of peril, the women of Jerusalem baked ritual cakes for the "queen of heaven," the goddess Ashtoreth, who, like the Babylonian goddess Ishtar, may have been symbolized in the heavens as a star. They believed she had more power than Israel's Lord (Yahweh) to avert disaster. (Jer. 7:18.) Some of Israel's greatest kings married non-Hebrew princesses who brought with them the worship of the goddess. Her worship continued despite the periodic efforts by the prophets and reformers to drive her out.

God's Bride

The ancient mother goddess was eventually repressed in Hebrew worship, but images associated with her survived in hidden or allegorical ways. We find this particularly in the idea that Israel, and especially Jerusalem, was the bride or spouse of God. The relationship of God and Israel was seen as a marriage. But, in the great prophets of the Old Testament, this nuptial imagery appeared only in a negative form. Israel, of course, could not be seen as a mother who encompasses her son-lover, as in Canaanite thought. Rather, Israel was a bride who was the child or creation of God. But she was a bride who was unfaithful to her divine husband. He had chosen her to be his own, but she played the harlot. She reverted to the worship of the old religions.

Thus the idea of Israel as God's spouse appeared in the Old

21

Testament primarily as a rival form of the marriage language of Baalism. The marriage language condemned that "harlotry" of Israel's worship of the gods of Canaan. The prophet Hosea particularly developed this theme:

> Then she shall say, "I will go
>   and return to my first husband,
>   for it was better with me then than now."
> And she did not know
>   that it was I who gave her
>   the grain, the wine, and the oil.
> . . . .
> And I will punish her for the feast days of the Baals
>   when she burned incense to them
> and decked herself with her ring and jewelry,
>   and went after her lovers,
>   and forgot me, says the LORD.
>
> *(Hos. 2:7–8, 13)*

The Song of Solomon

However, there is one writing in the Old Testament where the theme of marriage appears in a wholly positive light. It is The Song of Solomon. This book has often embarrassed interpreters of Scripture because of its frankly sensual imagery and delight in the pleasures of sexual love. The identity of the woman in the piece is unknown. Her lover is identified with Solomon, the king. The description of their beauty and attraction for each other is given in transfigured language. Reading it, we seem to be in a mysterious paradise. We are flooded with light and untouched by judgmental words.

The origin of The Song of Solomon is disputed. It seems to have been used simply as a popular wedding song. But the model for this song probably had its roots in the old poems of the love of the goddess and the king, which has been adapted to Hebrew tradition. The woman in the poem was not seen as a goddess, but only as a maiden of Jerusalem.

Nevertheless, the transfiguring of sensual delight, so typical of Canaanite religion, is preserved in this writing. It is interesting that interpreters of the Bible did not allow this poem to remain only as a human expression of love. To some extent, they also gave it a sacred meaning by interpreting it as an allegory of the marriage of Israel and God.

In the first century, when the canon of the Hebrew Scriptures was determined, Rabbi Akiba defended the place of The Song of Solomon in the canon by saying that its true meaning was the love of Israel and God. Rabbi Akiba said that it was the very "holy of holies" of Scripture. In this way the theme of a sacred marriage between God and Israel became profoundly enshrined in Jewish religious consciousness, despite its negative beginnings in the Prophets. Human marriages were to be modeled after this covenant of marriage between God and his beloved spouse. In contrast to the harlotry of Israel and Baal, marriage became the tender and intimate image for the relationship of God to his people.

For Thought and Discussion

1. As a result of the competition with Baalism, Old Testament religion understood the sexual unfaithfulness of a woman to her husband as a symbol of Israel's unfaithfulness to God. Is this a helpful image for us today? What problems do you see with this as an image of unfaithfulness to God?

2. In adopting the pagan concept of the sacred marriage, Biblical religion viewed sexual love between a man and a woman in marriage as an image of the love between God and his people. What do you think of this image? Is this a helpful way of thinking about the covenant between God and the human community? Is this a useful way to think about marriage? What problems do you see being created by this image? (See diagram on next page.)

23

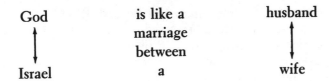

God ⭥ Israel — is like a marriage between a — husband ⭥ wife

3

MARY—THE WISDOM OF GOD

Proverbs, ch. 8

In the Wisdom Literature of Judaism another dimension of feminine symbolism appears in Jewish thought. The figure of Wisdom as a female personification of God appears in writings such as the Old Testament book of Proverbs. Not unlike the Christian concept of the Word, Wisdom is written about as though it were a second "person" of God who acts as a delegate of God the Father. In the Wisdom tradition, however, this second "person" of God is not male, but female. She is not a divine "son," but a divine "daughter."

Where did the writers of the Jewish Wisdom Literature of this period get this feminine image of God's Wisdom? We know that the mother goddesses among Israel's neighbors in the Near East and Egypt were commonly associated with Wisdom. The Babylonian goddess Ishtar was from earliest times regarded as a lawgiver, who brought divine wisdom down to mortal men. The Egyptian Isis especially is described as the embodiment of wisdom. In Egypt, Maat, or divine justice, was also seen as a feminine being who sprang forth from the sun god. As the daughter of the sun god, Maat expressed divine wisdom in ordering and governing the world. A similar idea probably lay behind the Greek myth that Athena was born from the head of Zeus and personified his wisdom.

Wisdom in the Old Testament

In the Old Testament, Wisdom is personified in Prov., ch. 8. Wisdom is described as the beloved daughter who existed with God at the creation of the world. She is a helper or agent through whom God creates the world. Proverbs 8:23, 27–30 says:

> Ages ago I was set up,
>> at the first, before the beginning of the earth. . . .
> When he established the heavens, I was there,
>> when he drew a circle on the face of the deep,
> when he made firm the skies above,
>> when he established the fountains of the deep,
> when he assigned to the sea its limit, . . .
> when he marked out the foundations of the earth,
>> then I was beside him, like a master workman;
> and I was daily his delight,
>> rejoicing before him always.

Wisdom is also seen as the agent through which God continually orders and governs the world, inscribing the created order with the pattern of the divine mind. Through her God is revealed to humans. She leads the souls of the wise back to communion with God. In theological language, Wisdom is God's agent in creation, providence, revelation, and redemption. She performs roles similar to that of the Logos or divine Word in Christian theology (compare John 1:1–18). However, she has no special human embodiment. Rather, she is the "spouse" or "bride" of wise men. In the book of Proverbs she can be seen as especially embodied in the ideal Jewish mother and wife who teaches her sons the ways of God (Prov. 8:32 to 9:12).

In the apocryphal book The Wisdom of Solomon, Wisdom is spoken of in more mystical language. She is compared to a "breath of the power of God, and a pure emanation of the glory of the Almighty" (Wisd. of Sol. 7:25). She is a self-manifestation or "image" of God. "She is a reflection of eternal light, a spotless mirror of the working of God, and an image of his goodness." (V. 26.) She is described as God's agent in the continual renewal of the world and in the revelation of God in human hearts. "While remaining in herself, she renews all things; in every generation she passes into holy souls and makes them friends of God, and prophets." (V. 27.) She is the beloved, or "bride," of the wise, especially of Solomon, the personification of the wise king. He says: "I loved her and sought her from my youth, and I desired to take her for my bride, and I became enamored of her beauty." (Ch. 8:2.)

Wisdom in Jewish Thought

During the period of the formation of the New Testament this emphasis on Wisdom seems to have been dropped from Jewish thought. This is probably because during this period the Wisdom image was taken up by a heretical movement called Gnosticism (the word comes from the Greek word "to know"). Gnosticism saw Wisdom as a kind of cosmic goddess through whom a fallen world was begotten and also the means by which souls would be redeemed from this fallen world. Some of this Wisdom speculation among the Gnostics may have found its way into early Christian thinking about Mother Church and may have influenced the growing theology of Mary. But Gnostic speculation was heretical for both Judaism and Christianity. Judaism also rejected Christian thinking about the divine Word of God, Jesus, God's Son. Wisdom speculation vanished from Judaism in this period.

However, in later Jewish writings the figure of divine Wisdom appears as a daughter of God, a bride of the wise and a mother of wise sons. She reappears in the image of the divine *Shekinah* (which means the Presence of God on earth; see Ex. 40:34–38; Num. 9:15–23). Like the word *sophia* (wisdom) in Greek, *shekinah* in Hebrew also is feminine in gender, and so encouraged thinking about the divine Presence as a feminine being. The idea of the divine Presence is in many ways similar to the Christian concept of the Holy Spirit. But Judaism thinks of this presence of the divine Spirit as a feminine, rather than as a masculine, being.

Bride of God

The "Presence of God" is herself divine; that is, she is an expression of God amid the creation. But rabbinic thinking also joined this concept of the "Presence of God" to another Biblical tradition that speaks of Israel as a wife or bride of God. (See, for example, Hos. 2:19–20.) Thus the feminine image of God's Presence has two dimensions. She is an expression of God. As such, she can be talked about as God's beloved daughter and also as his bride. She is also the collective embodiment of the people in their relationship to God. Here Israel "herself" is thought of as God's beloved wife. Israel as a collective being can also be seen as a mother who guides and nurtures her people, the children of Israel, bringing them back into friendship with God, their Father. The Jewish family thus becomes a mystical symbol for the family relations between God and Israel.

Rabbinic thought developed this concept of the "Divine Presence" into a drama that explained the plight of Israel after the fall of Jerusalem and the exile of the Jewish people among the Gentiles. God is pictured as having become separated from his people. The exile of Israel is the expression of this separation. Nevertheless God's beloved spouse, the *Shekinah* (Presence) remains with Israel. She accompanies the people of Israel into the exile, like a sorrowing mother who goes with her children after they have been estranged from their father. The exile, then, is in some sense a separation of God from himself; an estrangement of God from his own Spirit or Presence. The return from exile for Israel will also mean the overcoming of this estrangement of God from his bride, or his Presence.

In Jewish thought in the medieval period, speculation about the exile and the subsequent reconciliation of God and his Presence in Israel was given a very elaborate development. The sexual union of pious Jews with their wives, especially after the celebration of the Sabbath, was seen as a sacramental expression of the reunion of God with his wifely Presence.

The final union of God with Israel is anticipated on each Sabbath, when the Jewish community hails the advent of the Sabbath queen. The marriage union of God with Israel has now become a drama of redemption that will be completed only with the redemption of the world. A somewhat similar idea is found in the New Testament concept of the church at the end of history when it descends from heaven as a bride to be united with her husband, the Messiah (Rev. 21:2).

We have seen that in Old Testament thought the concept of a goddess was repressed. Yet in various ways the idea of a divine bride of God was reinstated. The community itself, in its covenant with God, could be seen as a spouse of God. This concept also lent itself to thinking of the community as a whole as a mother who mediates the commandments of God to the "sons" of Israel, her children. In the Wisdom tradition, Wisdom could be seen as a "daughter" or feminine expression of God active in Israel. Rabbinic speculation about the feminine *Shekinah* or Presence of God wove together both of these traditions. The drama of God's relations with his wifely Presence becomes a drama that explains the secret of the Fall and the redemption of Israel and the world.

For Thought and Discussion

1. In Christianity the divine Word and the Holy Spirit are both thought of as "masculine." The Word is typically spoken of as a "son." (See John, ch. 1, and Rom., ch. 8.)

   In Judaism, however, the somewhat similar concepts of God's Wisdom and God's Presence are both thought of as feminine. What difference do you think it would make, in prayer and religious experience, if one related to God's self-manifestations as feminine persons rather than masculine persons?

2. In Judaism the images of God's Wisdom and God's Presence as feminine beings were expressed in terms of a family-oriented religion. The relations of husband and wife, the relationship of the mother as mediator of social wisdom to her children, could be seen through the concept of the divine-human covenant. Do you think this "family" image is helpful for thinking about the divine-human relationship? What views of the family are reflected in this image of Israel as a wife and mother?

4

MARY—MOTHER OF JESUS

Luke 1:26 to 2:20; Matthew 1:18 to 2:23

The New Testament does not include much on the figure of Mary, the mother of Jesus, either as a historical figure or as a theological symbol. Paul does not refer to Mary by name at all. His only indirect reference to her is in Gal. 4:4, where he says that "when the time had fully come, God sent forth his Son, born of woman, born under the law." Paul does have a developed symbolism of the church as a feminine being (Eph. 5:21–33). But he never refers to Mary as a symbol of the church. This suggests that Mary had not become linked with the theology of the church in Paul's thought.

In Rev., ch. 12, there is a striking image of a woman crowned with stars who is in birth pangs with the Messiah. Traditionally this image has been linked to Mary. But there is no evidence that the author of the book linked the image of the woman to Jesus' historical mother. The woman here in Revelation is a symbol of the church in the time of persecution that is "pregnant" and in birth pangs with a Messianic king who is to come at some time in the future (i.e., the Second Coming of Christ).

References to Mary by name appear only in the Gospels and the book of Acts. In these writings references to her are of two different types: (1) the infancy narratives, which appear only in Luke and Matthew; and (2) the stories that describe the relations of Mary to Jesus' historical mission.

There seem to be some differences between these two traditions on which we may comment briefly.

Matthew's Narrative

Matthew's infancy narrative is actually quite different from Luke's, although we are used to reading them together. Matthew does not in fact make Mary an important figure at all. It is Joseph who is the central actor. It is he who receives the visit of the angel informing him of the miraculous nature of Jesus' birth. It is he who receives the second message from the angel telling him to take Mary and the child and flee to Egypt. In the genealogy that begins his gospel, Matthew traces the Davidic descent of Jesus through Joseph (Matt. 1:1–16).

The virgin birth is treated somewhat ambivalently by Matthew. Mary's pregnancy during the time of betrothal falls under suspicion of wrongdoing. Joseph is about to divorce her quietly when the angel tells him that she has conceived by the Holy Spirit. Mary is never the active person in Matthew's story. She is a passive instrument in a drama.

Luke's Narrative

Luke's infancy narrative conveys a different emphasis. Here Mary is the central figure. The angel's visit comes to her, not to Joseph. She is consulted in advance and gives her consent; thus she becomes an active, personal agent in the drama of God's incarnation. She goes to visit her cousin Elizabeth on her own initiative. At no time in these two events does she ask permission from her husband-to-be. Whereas Matthew merely reports that Jesus was born, Luke makes Mary the central actor in the birth (see Luke 2:7).

Mary's active meditation on the significance of the mission of her newborn son is stressed in Luke. After the revelation to the shepherds, he reports that "Mary kept all these things, pondering them in her heart" (v. 19). The prediction of Jesus' greatness by Simeon is addressed specifically to Mary (v. 34). When Jesus first manifests his wisdom in the Temple at the age of twelve, it is Mary who speaks out to admonish him (v. 48). After his reply, it is again said that Mary "kept all these things in her heart" (v. 51).

Luke makes Mary an active participant in the drama of Jesus' birth, accepting it through an act of free consent, and meditating upon the meaning of his future mission. Thus Luke begins that tradition which transforms Mary from being merely the historical mother of Jesus into an independent agent cooperating with God in the redemption of humanity. In other words, she begins to become a theological agent in her own right. This is expressed especially in her obedient consent to the divine command: "And Mary said, 'Behold, I am the handmaid of the Lord; let it be to me according to your word" (ch. 1:38).

In the Magnificat, Mary proclaims herself as the embodiment of Israel. She is God's betrothed rejoicing over her expected delivery by the Lord. Through her role she becomes a key figure in the history of God's work. "All generations will call me blessed; for he who is mighty has done great things for me." (Vs. 48–49.) She is the initial human agent in the unfolding of a divine revolution in history. She is the one through whom God has acted:

> He has scattered the proud in the imagination
> of their hearts,
> he has put down the mighty from their thrones,
> and exalted those of low degree;
> he has filled the hungry with good things,
> and the rich he has sent empty away.
> He has helped his servant Israel,
> in remembrance of his mercy.
>
> *(Vs. 51–54)*

In these passages Mary becomes much more than just a passive instrument of God. She becomes an active agent, cooperating with God through her personal will and consent to bring about the Messianic advent. She becomes a symbol of Israel, or the New Israel, the church, the redeemed people of God. See Acts, ch. 1. There she is placed alongside the apostles in the upper room at Pentecost. Thus it is from the Lucan tradition within the New Testament that we have the fountainhead of Mariology.

Virgin Birth

What is the meaning of the virgin birth in the infancy narratives? Both Matthew and Luke speak of Mary as a virgin and imply that the conception was miraculous. The form this idea takes in the New Testament is without precedent in Old Testament religion. The Old Testament speaks several times of special interventions of God in the births of the heroes of Israel, such as Isaac and Samuel. Since to be barren was the greatest disaster that could beset a woman, the greatest gift God could give her was to reverse this condition. This act of making a barren woman fertile becomes miraculous when God makes fertile the old or postmenopausal woman, as in the case of Sarah. But none of these interventions of God excludes the human father as biological parent. God does not "beget" the child, but makes the human sexual act effective or fertile.

It is possible that in the earliest Christian traditions the idea that God specially intervened in Jesus' birth also did not exclude the fatherhood of Joseph. The young Mary might have been thought of as a girl who is betrothed at too early an age to be fertile (a not uncommon practice at this time) and who conceives before menstruation gives the first evidence of her fertility. Rabbinic writings refer to such births as "virgin births." So God's miraculous intervention does not need to exclude Joseph's biological role. At least some of the traditions that shaped the New Testament clearly believed Joseph to be Jesus' biological father. Otherwise there would be no point in the genealogy recorded by Matthew that traces

Jesus' Davidic ancestry through Joseph. We know that some groups of Jewish Christians in the early centuries of the church, such as the Ebionites, continued to regard Jesus as the divinely chosen, but natural, son of Joseph.

In the two New Testament infancy narratives Joseph's natural fatherhood has been replaced by a miraculous begetting before Mary has any sexual relations with her husband-to-be. This is clearly the intent of Matthew's narrative, which says explicitly: "He took his wife, but knew her not until she had borne a son" (Matt. 1:24–25).

An important influence on this Christian tradition was probably the Greek version of the Old Testament, used by Christians, which translated the Messianic prediction of Isa. 7:14: "Behold, a virgin shall conceive." (See Matt. 1:23.) In the original Hebrew of this passage the word used meant "young woman," whereas the Greek word that translated it meant specifically a woman who had not known any sexual relations ("virgin").

However, the theological meaning of the virgin birth in the New Testament infancy narratives is substantially the same as that of the Old Testament's divine interventions in the births of great heroes of Israel. Thus such a person is divinely chosen from birth as an agent of God, by a special act of God in his conception. Applied to Jesus, it is a dramatic way of saying that he is "elected" by God from his mother's womb. His birth is a special act of divine blessing upon a person designated to play a unique role in God's plan of salvation.

There is no suggestion in the New Testament that the virgin birth implies some special superiority of virginity over marriage or that sexual relations are evil. In other words, the virgin birth is a statement about Jesus, not about Mary. It is an assertion about his special, divine "chosenness" from the moment of his conception. It is not a declaration of Mary's superior status as a virgin. There is no suggestion in the New Testament that Mary remained a virgin. Indeed, Matthew specifically implies that after the birth of Jesus, Mary and Joseph had normal marital relations. The Gospels also imply that Mary was the mother of other sons and daughters. (See Mark 6:3 and Matt. 13:55–56.) The virgin birth stories do not suggest an exalted status for Mary. Rather, the story of the virgin birth is told against a background that continues to imply that, otherwise, she was a normal married woman.

For Thought and Discussion

1. The Bible uses the idea of a special intervention in the conception of a child to denote that the child is especially favored by God and chosen for a high destiny. In what way do we today think of a person as specially chosen for a high destiny? How would we today illustrate the idea that God has chosen someone for a special role "from the mother's womb"?

2. The picture painted of Mary in Luke's infancy narrative has many elements. What elements in it suggest a conventional portrait of the loving mother and dutiful wife? What elements in it are unconventional and suggest surprising attributes for a woman in Jewish society at Jesus' time?

5
MARY
AND THE MISSION OF JESUS

Mark 3:31–35; Matthew 12:46–50;
Luke 8:19–21; John 2:1–11; 19:25–27

In the infancy narratives of the New Testament Jesus' Messianic identity is revealed to Mary and Joseph from the beginning. They become active cooperators in the divine mission. In other sections of the Gospels, Mary and Jesus' family are unbelievers who stand aside from and even oppose his mission. The hometown people of Nazareth, who know his father, mother, sisters, and brothers, are presented as unreceptive and hostile to his teaching. (Matt. 13:53–58; Mark 6:1–6; Luke 4:16–30.) Jesus' family tries to seize him, believing him to be mad. (Mark 3:21, TEV.)

At one point Jesus' mother and brothers come to speak to him. Jesus takes the occasion of their arrival to repudiate loyalty to his family in favor of kinship with his disciples. (Matt. 12:48–50.)

Rejection of the Family

Jesus' preaching is marked by a negativity toward the kinship group. He remarked that those who would be saved must be ready to fall into conflict with their parents, brothers, sisters, and spouse, to depart from their families to join the fellowship of believers. (Luke 12:49–53.) Luke also records a saying in which Jesus rejects honoring his mother because she has borne such a son. The woman in the crowd who cries, "Blessed is the womb that bore you, and the breasts that you

37

sucked!" receives the reply, "Blessed rather are those who hear the word of God and keep it!" (Ch. 11:27–28.)

This negativity would seem to reflect, in part, the actual experience between Jesus and his family. In the Synoptic Gospels, Mary does not appear either at the cross or in the resurrection stories. In these accounts of Jesus' death and resurrection, it is not his mother but his female disciples, Mary Magdalene, Salome, and Mary, the mother of James the Less, who are faithful to him and receive the first revelation of his resurrection. Jesus' mother and brothers seem to be unbelievers during his lifetime.

In the book of Acts and the letters of Paul, however, we have evidence that the family became disciples at the time of his death or shortly thereafter. Luke places the mother and brothers, along with the Twelve and Jesus' female disciples, in the upper room at Pentecost. (Acts 1:13–14.) Mary subsequently vanishes from the historical record of Acts. But Jesus' brother James became the prominent leader in the Jerusalem church by the time of Paul's ministry. (See Acts, ch. 15, and Gal., ch. 2.) He stood for a faithful, Pharisaic, Jewish Christianity, against Paul's revaluation of the law.

The exact history of the relations of Jesus' mother and brothers to later Christianity is obscure. But it would seem that it included both a hostility within Jesus' lifetime and a divisive influence within the church after his death.

John's Gospel

John relates two stories about Mary that are not found in the Synoptics, and that appear to be more favorable to Mary. In John 2:1–11, Jesus performs his first miracle at Cana at Mary's request. Furthermore, John alone includes Jesus' mother at the crucifixion, along with her sister, Mary the wife of Clopas, and Mary Magdalene (ch. 19:25). But when these stories are looked at in the context of John's theology, rather than through the eyes of later Christian piety and art, the impression that they exalt Mary somewhat disappears. John's

Gospel is built on the contrast between the fleshly level of reality, where all is blindness and disbelief, and the spiritual level of redeeming insight. The Jews, Jesus' family, and even the disciples are foils of the realm of darkness and unbelief against which the drama of revelation is played out.

The story of the miracle at Cana reflects these two levels. Jesus' miracle is a sign that the old waters of purification, i.e., the Jewish law, have been superseded by the "new wine" of the gospel. Mary's role reflects a double meaning. Belonging to the world of his fleshly kinship, she sees the matter literally. Jesus' harsh response to her: "O woman, what have you to do with me?" (ch. 2:4) indicates her lack of understanding of the inner meaning he is about to reveal through his response to her request.

Mary at the Cross

Recent Roman Catholic thought has seen the figure of Mary at the cross in John's Gospel as an indication that she is the symbol of the church and is even a "co-offerer" of the sacrifice at Golgotha with him. But nothing in John's account suggests such an exalted view. Rather, it would seem that here, as at Cana, Mary represents the Old Israel. John is presented as Jesus' heir and the embodiment of the spiritual people. Jesus' mother after the flesh is presented to the heir of Jesus' spiritual sonship to show that here the fleshly Israel passes over into the custody of the spiritual Israel. (Ch. 19: 25–27.)

But John does not make Mary a witness of the resurrection. Here, as in the Synoptic Gospels, Mary Magdalene is the central figure. John indeed stresses their intimacy. (See ch. 20:11–18.)

Mary Magdalene—An Unconventional Woman

In the Synoptics, Mary Magdalene and the other female disciples of Jesus play the central role. They remained faithful to Jesus at the cross and the tomb. The male disciples betrayed him and ran away. The women were rewarded for this faithfulness by being the first witnesses of the resurrection. Mary, Jesus' mother, was not included.

The later history of these traditions about Mary Magdalene is rather obscure. On the one hand, there arose in the second century, and perhaps even earlier, heretical Gnostic traditions that exalted Mary Magdalene as the specially beloved disciple of Jesus. She is seen as the one who received the highest revelation of the meaning of the resurrection. The right of women to equal place among the disciples is defended through her.

On the other hand, the orthodox Christian church seems to have suppressed the role of Mary Magdalene. She is portrayed in the tradition as a former harlot. Actually there is nothing in the New Testament to confirm this idea. It came about through a confusion of the stories about Mary Magdalene with several other stories about women, such as the story of Mary of Bethany who anoints Jesus (John 12:1–8), the unknown former sinner who anoints Jesus in Luke 7:36–50, and the story of the woman taken in adultery (John 8:1–11).

The suppression of the role of Mary Magdalene in the official church tradition may have something to do with the desire of the church to assign subordinate and conventional roles to women. Whatever her sexual history, Mary Magdalene is clearly an unconventional woman. Here is an independent woman whose close relations with Jesus are borne out by her faithfulness at the cross and her primacy in the resurrection experience. She represents a role model for women that later church leaders probably preferred to neglect!

Mary—A Conventional Woman

In the later church tradition Jesus again comes to have a faithful woman at his side, a woman who understands him from the beginning and remains loyal to him to the end, a

40

woman who especially cooperates with him in the drama of salvation and mediates it to others. This woman is not Mary Magdalene, but his mother, Mary of Nazareth. By replacing Mary Magdalene with Mary, the mother, as the "woman who loved him," the church replaced a dangerously unconventional role model with a conventional role model and relationship.

Mary, the mother, is a proper role model for both the Christian virgin and the Christian mother. She is the chaste virgin and also the loving mother who senses Jesus' greatness from the beginning. She silently supports him with her prayers and finally appears beside him at the final agony of the cross. This is the picture of Mary the mother that Luke begins to create in his infancy narrative and that is completed by the later tradition of the church. Mother's love is a safe love, both for women and for the church's image of Jesus.

However there are within the New Testament many indications that the facts about Mary, Jesus' mother, are otherwise. The mother does not seem to be a follower during Jesus' lifetime. She is even hostile to his mission. It is the woman disciple, Mary Magdalene, who puts to shame not only the family but also the male disciples by her faith and her steadfastness at the final time of crisis. These facts must make us put a question mark beside the tradition of Mary, Jesus' mother, as the woman who best represents "the church."

For Thought and Discussion

1. Read I Tim. 2:8–15. What role is prescribed for women in the church here? What woman would be preferred by this church? The Mary of Matthew's infancy story? The Mary of Luke's infancy story? Mary Magdalene?

2. In the Gospels there seems to be a tension between the kinship group or family and the "church," i.e., the followers of Jesus. Think about other groups or movements that

seem to draw people into an opposition to their families. List some such movements. What role do they play in people's development? What is the difference between a church modeled after the family and a church modeled after such movements in tension with the family?

6

MARY
AND THE FEMININITY OF GOD

Ephesians 5:21–33

The use of feminine symbols was not unusual in the Old Testament or in Judaism. Our study has shown that such images as Israel as God's bride, Israel as a mother, and God's Wisdom personified as a feminine being were quite traditional. The early Christian church inherited these feminine symbols and continued to use them. At first they were adapted and developed in the New Israel quite independent of teaching about Mary as an individual. Later as Mariology developed, they were drawn in and absorbed by it. Mariology, therefore, consists partly in focusing these feminine symbols on the person of the mother of Jesus.

The feminine symbols describe three kinds of relationships with God: (1) the believing community is seen as God's feminine companion; (2) an aspect of God at work in his creation—his Spirit, Presence, or Wisdom—can be received as feminine; and (3) the feminine can symbolize the soul's openness and receptivity to God's initiatives.

We shall look at each of these to see how they appeared in early church tradition.

Mother Church, Bride of Christ

The most important feminine symbol in Christianity is the church as "bride" of Christ and "mother" of Christians. This idea came from the Old Testament image of Israel as God's bride. But there is an important difference in the Christian development of this image. The Old Testament used the image both as an ideal and also as a criticism of Israel's failure to live up to this ideal. (See Hos., ch. 2.) Now the church is seen as the redeemed bride of the Messianic age. Ephesians, ch. 5, contains the most extended imagery of the church as Messianic bride:

> Christ loved the church and gave himself up for her, that he might sanctify her, having cleansed her by washing of water with the word, that he might present the church to himself in splendor, without spot or wrinkle. *(Vs. 25–27)*

The union of Christ and the church is still incomplete, however. In the book of Revelation the church is seen as a pregnant woman who is in birth pangs with the Messiah and flees into the wilderness, pursued by the dragon of evil. The church is symbolized as a woman who wears the sun for her mantle, standing on the moon with a crown of twelve stars. (Rev. 12:1–6.) After the conquest of the evil beast the church descends like a bride to be joined in sacred marriage with the Messianic King. (Ch. 21:2.)

This symbol of the church as bride and mother continues in the writings of the church fathers. The church is seen as a "virginal" mother who bears virginal children. These belong to the new age of the spirit, where there is no more marrying or giving in marriage. The milk with which she nourishes them is wisdom. The waters of baptism are seen as the church's womb of rebirth, fertilized by the power of the Holy Spirit.

The church can be seen as the new Eve, as Christ is the new Adam. As Eve was created out of the side of Adam, so the church is born of water and blood from the side of Christ on Calvary (John 19:34; water and blood stand for Baptism and the Lord's Supper). The marriage of Christ and the church is the union that brings forth reborn Christian souls. Baptism is the rebirth from sin and death to immortal life.

The church's children are virginal offspring who reject physical marriage. Thus in some strange way the spiritualizing of marriage and motherhood also became a rejection of physical sexuality and motherhood. The church as the divine mother of eternal life is a rejection of the human mother.

Wisdom: The Femininity of God

In the Wisdom tradition we have found the idea of Wisdom as the daughter of God, helpmeet in Creation and revelation, and bride of the wise. This idea is not prominent in the Latin theology of the Western church although Mary is to be identified with *Sapientia* and accordingly was called "Seat of Wisdom." Wisdom, however, becomes a favorite theme in Eastern Orthodoxy. The "Mother Church" of Constantinople is named Hagia Sophia (Holy Wisdom). It symbolizes the ideas of Wisdom as God's feminine Presence and the church as the maternal womb of reborn Christians.

The modern Russian Orthodox theologian Sergius Bulgakov has developed the Eastern theology of Wisdom. Wisdom is seen as the all-encompassing divine ground of being out of which the Trinity emerges. It creates the world, guides it to perfection, and unites the creation with its Creator. Such a theology of Wisdom restates in some ways the ancient theology of the "world egg" (see Chapter 1). Wisdom is not just to be identified with one of the persons of the Trinity, such as the Word or the Spirit. Wisdom is the ground of being of the three persons of God.

Wisdom's being is made visible in the maternity of Mary. Wisdom governs the whole process of creation and redemption from beginning to end. Complete redeemed humanity is found, not in Jesus alone, but in Jesus encompassed by Mary. Together they reveal the full mystery of Creation.

Speaking of Mary, Bulgakov says:

In the Virgin there are united Holy Wisdom and the Wisdom of the created world, the Holy Spirit and human hypostasis [the

45

created person]. Her body is completely spiritual and transfigured. She is the justification, the end, the meaning of creation; she is, in this sense, the glory of the world. In her, God is already all in all. *(From* The Wisdom of God, *by Sergius Bulgakov, quoted in* The Virgin Mary, *by Giovanni Miegge. Lutterworth Press, 1955)*

This kind of Wisdom theology is not usually found in Western thought, but some theologians did refer to Jesus as a mother. Jesus is seen as a nurturing figure who feeds us on his own body. In the fourteenth century the female mystic, Julian of Norwich, brought this idea of Jesus' maternity to its fullest expression. Julian always speaks of God as both mother and father and also of Jesus as a mother. Julian says that the power of the Trinity is our Father, but the Wisdom of the Trinity is our Mother, through whom we have our rebirth. Jesus is a brother and spouse of the soul:

Jesus Christ, who doeth good against evil, is our very Mother. We have our being of him, there, where the ground of Motherhood beginneth. . . . As truly as God is our Father, so truly is God our Mother. *(From* The Revelations of Divine Love of Julian of Norwich, *tr. by James Walsh; Harper & Row, Publishers, Inc., 1961)*

The Virgin Soul as Bride of Christ

Christian mystical writers often speak of the soul as the bride of Christ. (The word "psyche" [soul] is feminine in Greek and was traditionally represented in mythology as a maiden goddess.) The human soul may thus be seen as "feminine," as a passive, receptive self in relationship to the higher "masculine" divine action upon the soul. In this relationship, the soul is viewed as a virgin bride who ecstatically awaits the visitation of Christ, the divine bridegroom.

The Song of Solomon became the primary Scriptural text for this mystical tradition of the soul's bridal communion with Christ. The rabbis in the first century had already interpreted this poem as the marriage hymn of Yahweh and Israel.

In the early third century after Christ, the Christian theologian Origen interpreted The Song of Solomon to mean the marriage of the church with Christ. But he found its deeper meaning on the mystical level as the marriage of the soul with the divine Word.

Throughout the Middle Ages, The Song of Solomon provided the texts for monastic meditation and commentaries on the mystical quest and the communion of the soul with God. The writing of the Spanish Catholic mystic John of the Cross brought this tradition of spiritual marriage to its highest point of development. Every detail of the poem is made to provide aspects of the soul's journey into fuller and more complete communion with God.

The Song of Solomon is the one piece of Biblical literature largely written from the viewpoint of the female person. It is the expectant bride who speaks, describing her hopes, fears, and experiences of love. This perspective of the poem allows the mystic to speak fulsomely of the subjective side of mystical experience. This is different from the official theology, which speaks objectively about God's work on behalf of the soul's salvation. The soul, active as a female, aspiring self, speaks of God as a lover for whom the soul longs, and whom the soul experiences as God comes to her.

FOR THOUGHT AND DISCUSSION

1. Ask each member of the group to draw a picture of his or her "soul" (mind, ego) in relationship to the body. What kind of image of the soul appears and how is it related to the body? Is it like a child? Is it like a parent? Is it male or female?

2. Each person may also want to draw a picture of the soul or self in relation to God. Again, what kind of person is the soul, and how is the relationship between the two pictured? Show the pictures to the group. Ask each person to discuss what he or she was trying to say with the

pictures. Ask other persons to reflect on what each person has drawn.

Conclusion to Part I

In this chapter and in the earlier chapters we have tried to show the development of feminine religious imagery in the cultures that came into Christianity: ancient Near Eastern, Jewish, and Greek. We have shown that from earliest times these cultures pictured God and the relationship to God in feminine as well as masculine terms. Neither a male nor a female symbol was entirely lost. Each was translated and reinterpreted in new ways in the Old Testament and then in Christianity.

All of this is important for understanding the background of teaching about Mary. For Mariology does not come so much from a striking religious experience of Mary herself by the first Christians. Mariology is a later development that uses the figure of the mother of Jesus as the person around whom to regroup this theology of feminine experience. In the following chapters we shall show the kinds of ideas that began to develop as Christians continued to reflect on Mary as a theological symbol.

Part II

MARY IN THE CHURCH

INTRODUCTION

The development of Marian symbols in the church's tradition flows from a blending of different sources. Such symbols as the church as virgin bride of Christ and mother of Christians were attached to Mary. Through this door more remote images from the goddesses of antiquity (which were discussed in the first chapter) entered indirectly. Gentile converts to Christianity transferred to Mary the devotion they had once given to the pagan mother of the gods and the queen of heaven. Furthermore, Marian doctrine evolved out of Mary's role as mother of Jesus, the incarnate One. As teaching about Christ developed, Mariology followed by way of analogy. Mariology has acted as an extension and safeguard of the doctrines of Christ's uniqueness.

In the next three chapters we shall sketch the development of Marian doctrines. We hope to make clear the basic lines of development and the theological meaning behind the different doctrines. This will provide a basis for understanding the Protestant criticism of this development. Finally, we shall ask what this tradition means to us today and how it may help us to understand the problems of women in the church.

The major Marian doctrines are: (1) the New Eve; (2) the Perpetual Virgin; (3) the Mother of God; (4) the Assumption; (5) the Mediator of Grace; and (6) the Immaculate Conception.

51

We will divide this development into three historical periods:

1. Early developments—second to fourth centuries

2. The establishment of Mariology—fifth to twelfth centuries

3. The flowering of Mariology—late Middle Ages to Counter-Reformation Catholicism

Protestants who once reacted negatively to this development are now called upon to understand Mariology and to find positive aspects in the teaching for the contemporary church.

7
MARY—
NEW EVE
AND PERPETUAL VIRGIN

The apostolic tradition through the mid-second century ignores Mary as a theological symbol. Beginning with the writings of the Christian apologist Justin Martyr, around A.D. 155, and continuing with the works of the church fathers Tertullian and Irenaeus at the end of the century, we find the symbol of the "new Eve" applied to Mary. The new Eve (Mary) embodies believing Israel, obedient to God's will. She parallels Christ, the new Adam.

The symbol of the church as the new Eve also existed independently of Mariology. Since Mary is the historical mother of Jesus and the church is the daughter-bride of Christ and the mother of reborn Christians, the identification of Mary with the church creates a confusion of symbolic sexual relations that is typical of Mariology ever since. She is historically mother of Christ but, like the church, also the daughter and bride of Christ.

The church fathers of the second century did not allow themselves to become too fanciful about this analogy of Mary and the church. They remained soberly rooted in Luke's annunciation story. Thus Mary, through her "Let it be to me according to your word" (Luke 1:38), became the first believer. She represents believing Israel and is the link between the Old Israel and the New. She, the daughter of the Old Israel, is the first member of the new covenant. She depicts the new believing community of people who accept the

Word of God, in contrast to the old Eve and her fallen offspring, who rejected God's commandment. Mary is seen as having reversed the evil work of Eve. Through her obedience, she brings forth Jesus through whom the sin of fallen humanity is to be overcome.

Irenaeus, for example, writing about A.D. 185, believed that each of the elements in the history of the Fall (Gen., ch. 3) had a parallel in the history of salvation, one that overcame and reversed that element. The virgin Eve was misled by an angelic being and disobeyed God, causing the fall of humanity. So the salvation of humanity must come about by a second virgin (Mary) who received a true word from an angel and obediently accepted God's word.

The Perpetual Virginity of Mary

In the second century there arose a heretical movement called Gnosticism which rejected the goodness of marriage and the creation. Gnosticism exalted the virgin as the true Christian. The church fathers rejected these views, but by the middle of the fourth century these ideas began to be accepted by bishops and teachers of the church, at least on the level of popular piety. The result was a contradiction between the theology of the church, which said that creation was good, and a piety which suggested that it was bad. An enthusiasm for the monastic life developed from such popular piety.

Asceticism provided two impulses toward the development of Marian doctrine. First, there was the desire to safeguard Jesus' birth from any relation to sexual intercourse. Second, Mary's virginity itself became exalted as a symbol of the calling to Christian virginity.

Mary's virginity can be defined in different stages. First, she can be said to have been a virgin in the actual conception of Jesus. Second, she can be said to have remained a virgin in the birth of Jesus (with unbroken hymen). And third, she can be said to have remained a virgin for the rest of her life. The second-century church fathers accepted the first view of virginity but not necessarily the other two. Tertullian, for example, denied that Mary's hymen remained unbroken in the birth. He also assumed that the brothers and sisters of Jesus mentioned in the gospels were children of Mary and Joseph, born after Jesus.

These further views of Mary's virginity (unbroken hymen and perpetual virginity) are first found in the Protevangelium of James. In this apocryphal infancy story dated as early as A.D. 150, Mary is a vowed Temple virgin from her childhood. She is given into the hands of the aged Joseph, who is to be her guardian. He is a widower with grown children (making the siblings of the Jesus of the Gospels half brothers and sisters, children of Joseph by a former marriage). One of these half brothers, James, known in the New Testament as "the Lord's brother," purports to be the writer of the Protevangelium. This writing claims to provide an eyewitness account of Mary's virginal delivery of Jesus.

The story shows that Jesus was born by passing through Mary's hymen without breaking it. This idea is modeled after the postresurrection story in which Jesus passed through closed doors without opening them (John 20:19–29). Salome, the midwife, is the "doubting Thomas" who refuses to believe that a woman has delivered and remained a virgin. "Unless I put forth my finger and test her condition, I will not believe that a virgin has brought forth." Salome discovers that the hymen indeed is still intact. Her unbelief is forthwith punished by searing pain and a withered limb until she prays for forgiveness and testifies to her faith.

Tertullian was acquainted with a version of this writing. He rejected the doctrine of the unbroken hymen because it suggested the Gnostic view that Jesus did not have a real physical body but only a spiritual body that could pass through the doors of the womb without opening it. However, two centuries later, another church father, Jerome, accepted this idea of Mary's remaining a virgin though giving birth by referring specifically to this analogy with the risen Lord's passing through closed doors.

Defense of Asceticism

In the late fourth century an argument over these doctrines broke out in a new form. Helvidius and Jovinian, two church-men, one a former monk, objected to the new doctrines of the monks that denigrated marriage. They rejected the ideas that virginity was better than marriage and that the truly con-verted Christian should live in sexual abstinence. They argued that marriage and virginity were of equal worth as Christian vocations. They took Mary as their model for this, because she was a virgin at Jesus' conception, but afterward lived as a married woman and had sons and daughters by Joseph. Thus she sanctified both states of life.

Two important church leaders at this time, Ambrose and Jerome, were outraged at this suggestion that Mary was not permanently a virgin. By implication this also suggested to them that virginity was not the primary standard of Christian virtue. Both wrote strong letters against Jovinian and Hel-vidius. In his tract against Helvidius, Jerome worked out an exegesis of the Gospels that made the "brothers and sisters" of Jesus into "cousins." Mary was a perpetual virgin. This still continues to be accepted by the Roman Catholic tradition and by many Protestants.

From reading this tract it is clear that Jerome's chief pur-pose was the defense of ascetic doctrine. He wanted to defend the absolute superiority of virginity. He believed that sexual intercourse was debasing, even in marriage. Mary, for him, was the symbol of unblemished virginity untouched by carnal relations. She symbolized the "new creature" of heavenly redemption, where all will be like angels and there will be no marrying or giving in marriage. (See Matt. 22:30.) Marriage is still allowed in the Christian era, but it is no longer norma-tive. The blessings of God upon childbearing have been re-scinded, because the Christian already lives in the age to come and the end of the present finite world is drawing near. To Jerome, Jesus, Mary, and Joseph were all virgins.

Thus Jerome cannot say that Mary, the model of virginity, could relapse into the inferior state of marriage, sexual relations, and childbearing. The true followers of the Lamb are those who have not defiled their virgin state (Rev. 14:4). Jerome's defense of Mary's perpetual virginity is based on this view of the Christian calling. The "first family" of the New Testament, therefore, must be models of this state of life for other Christians.

FOR THOUGHT AND DISCUSSION

1. The early idea of the "new Eve" seems to have been based on the fact that humanity was created male and female and fell from original purity through the acts of both a man and a woman. Therefore, both man and woman must have a new start. If there is a new Adam, there must also be a new Eve. What do you think of this idea?

2. In the early church, marriage was linked to mortal life, and virginity was seen as symbolizing a dedication to the higher life, which is immortal.

   How would you today try to symbolize such a life dedicated to those things which are eternal? Is there some completely different way of relating "mortal life" and "eternal life"?

8

MARY—GOD'S MOTHER!

In the late fourth century, after the Christian church had been established as the exclusive religion of the Roman Empire by the Emperor Theodosius, teaching about Mary developed very rapidly. Masses of people who came into the Christian church brought with them their former devotion to the mother goddess. Churches were often dedicated to Mary on or near the site of a former temple of the goddess. The image of the seated virgin with the baby Jesus in her lap was taken from the traditional image of the Egyptian goddess Isis, with the baby god-king Horus enthroned on her knees. It became a favorite image in Christian art. Symbols for the new queen of heaven were borrowed from the earlier queens: the mural crown of Cybele and the stars and moon of Isis.

Mary also was pressed into being a patron of agricultural fertility. From the fifth century on, feasts of Mary duplicated the high points of the traditional cycle of the year: the feasts of sowing, harvesting, and vintage in mid-May (the Feast of Mary's Queenship); mid-August (the Feast of the Assumption); and originally for some December (the Feast of the Annunciation). Christ's birthday, fixed on December 25, was on the feast day of the winter solstice, the birth of the invincible sun (patron of the emperors).

Marian devotion appears on two levels. There is the Mary of the official theology and of the monks, which venerate her as the virgin who was docilely obedient to the divine will. So

58

doctrines about her were shaped in an antisexual mold. But there is also the Mary of the people who is still the earth mother. She is venerated for her helping power in natural crises. She helps the woman through birth pangs, the farmer's cow through delivery. Like the goddesses of old, she assures the coming of the new rains, the new grain, the new lamb. She is the maternal image of the divine who understands the daily needs of ordinary people and who renews the processes of nature upon which they depend for life. In this sketch of Mariology we are emphasizing the first kind of Mariology, but even today the devotion to Mary among Catholic peasants is founded more on the second.

Mary as Mother of God

The most controversial doctrinal struggle in the fifth century took place over the title "Mother of God." The title was probably first used among Egyptian theologians in the fourth century. But the school of Scripture in Antioch in the Middle East, represented by Theodore of Mopsuestia and later by Nestorius, was suspicious of the title. Nestorius suggested instead that Mary should be called "Mother of Christ." She is mother of Jesus' humanity but not of the divine Word.

The argument revolved around a fine point of Christological doctrine: namely, whether the human and divine natures in Jesus had mingled to the point where one could speak of his human mother also as mother of God, since the human son was also God.

The opponents of the title wanted the unity of Christ defined in such a way as to cause no confusion between the human nature and the divine nature. The issue was also heated up by church rivalry between the Egyptians, who supported the "Mother of God" title, and the church of Antioch, which supported "Mother of Christ." At a church council in Ephesus in A.D. 431 the Egyptians took control, threw out Nestorius (who had been elected patriarch of Constantinople), and declared their own views.

59

This victory of the Egyptians was shortlived. In A.D. 451, Leo I, the bishop of Rome, offered a formula that incorporated Nestorius' concern for a clear distinction between the two natures and also accepted the principle that Jesus' divine and human natures mingled. Then one could use divine titles to refer to his human nature and vice versa. On this ground, the title "Mother of God" was accepted.

Mary Carried Divine Power

Popular piety took the title "Mother of God" and developed dramatic ideas about Mary herself. In the apocryphal Gospel of Bartholomew, written in the early fifth century, we read the following story: At one time the apostles begged Mary, Jesus' mother, to describe the divine conception by which God, "whom the heavens could not contain" descended into her. She says she cannot describe it, because if she does, fire will come out of her mouth and the whole earth will be consumed. But the apostles continue to beg her. She tells them to hold her on all sides. Otherwise her limbs will fly apart in telling the terrible mystery of how the Creator came down to occupy her mortal frame.

She then begins the story of the angel's pronouncement. But as she starts to describe the experience of the incarnation itself, fire comes out of her mouth. Only Jesus' timely appearance from heaven prevents the whole creation from being burned up.

In this popular story, it is clear that Mary's maternity is not seen as a humble bearing of Jesus' humanity. It is the birthing of the divine power through which the world itself was created.

The enormous emotion generated by this dispute in the fifth century also suggests that more was at stake than a fine point of Christological definition. The definition of Mary as mother of God was the opening wedge for her veneration as a substitute mother goddess. However much theology might narrow this view in theory, popular piety would widen it in

60

imagination. It is not accidental that the declaration of this title at the Council of Ephesus took place amid scenes of fanatical enthusiasm by the populace of a city that had once given its enthusiastic support to another virgin mother, the great Artemis of Ephesus. (See Acts, ch. 19.)

The Assumption

From Egypt also came the story of Mary's assumption, i.e., of her being carried bodily to heaven after her death. In the New Testament Apocrypha there are. two different versions of Mary's death and afterlife. In "The Falling Asleep of Mary," by Pseudo-John the Evangelist, Mary's body is carried away by angels to be preserved intact with the other saints in the terrestrial paradise until the general resurrection. Only her soul is carried up to heaven. Although she was marked by special honor, this story says nothing more about Mary's death than was believed about the other holy ones.

In a second version of the story, the Transitus Mariae, by Pseudo-Melito, Mary's body is resurrected by Jesus after her death and carried to heaven. Earlier Biblical traditions had pointed to other worthies, such as Enoch and Moses (see Gen. 5:24 and Jude 9), who had been carried bodily to heaven. When these apocryphal texts appeared in the West in the late fifth century, they were sufficiently foreign to known tradition to be condemned by Pope Gelasius I (A.D. 492–496).

Both versions of the story of the assumption continued to be current in the West in the Middle Ages. In the ninth century, two writings, one ascribed to Jerome and the other to Augustine, took different views of the matter. Pseudo-Jerome took the view that Mary's fate after her death was unknown. Pseudo-Augustine asserted that her virginal state must have meant that her body was preserved incorrupt and was taken to heaven. In the later Middle Ages the second view came to be favored. Both opinions continued to be espoused by various Catholic theologians until the view favoring Mary's bodily assumption into heaven gained the ascendancy and was decided by papal decree in 1950.

Queen of Angels and Saints

The idea of Mary's assumption has considerable religious importance. As a parallel to the ascension of Jesus (who, in the early tradition, also is said to have been "taken up" into heaven, not to have risen by his own power—Acts 2:32–33), Mary now becomes available in heaven as an object of prayer and devotion. She is not just a figure of past history. She is established above space and time in a transcendent realm where she is present at all times and places. She is the queen of angels and saints. In her assumption she comes to be seen as enthroned on the right hand of Christ to reign over the heavenly congregation. This is a favorite theme in Christian art.

Mary's assumption also means that she is the first of the saints to participate in the resurrection of the body. She anticipates and prefigures the church of the general resurrection at the end of time. Again we can see a duplication of a doctrine about Christ. In the New Testament it is Christ who is the "first fruits" of the general resurrection. However, as Christ comes to be more and more removed from human nature, the doctrines about him cease to be symbols of the redemption of humanity. Teachings about Mary develop as parallels to doctrines about Christ and indicate that Mary is a new symbolic figure who provides the redemption of humanity. Christ thus comes to be seen primarily as the representative of God, and so no longer really represents humanity. Mary takes his place as the symbol of the hope of the human race for final salvation.

FOR THOUGHT AND DISCUSSION

1. What are the implications of the Gospel of Bartholomew story that Mary, when she describes the incarnation of

Jesus through her, breathes fire from her mouth? How is this a useful symbol of the power of God in her?

2. Both the ascension of Christ and the assumption of Mary (the symbol of the church) represent the promise of the final resurrection of humanity. Do we need two symbols for the resurrection? Can you think of other ways of representing the idea that our final resurrection is prepared for us and already fulfilled "in principle"?

9

MARY—GRACE AND GOODNESS

In medieval theology Mary becomes the representative of redeemed humanity, purified of sin, the heart of the church, the New Israel, the queen of the heavenly congregation, and the firstfruits of the general resurrection. From the twelfth through the fifteenth centuries her star rises in medieval theology, her glory growing ever brighter in inverse proportion to the downgrading of real women. As indicated in the preceding chapter, this development of devotion to Mary is partly a reaction to the removal of the human from Christ, who is seen primarily as the stern judge of the Final Judgment.

Later medieval thought also devotes much attention to the crucified Christ as a figure of agony. But here too he is a terifying figure who condemns unforgivable human guilt. Christ stands primarily for punishment of guilt and judgment. The paradox of the just and merciful God is dissolved into divine wrath (Jesus) and a human woman (Mary) representing mercy. She, like an understanding mother, can make allowances for the inadequacies of human nature. As Christ becomes more to be feared, trust is transferred to Mary. Devotion to her can guarantee that even the worst sinner has a chance of salvation. A mother's heart is much too tender to allow even the most wayward child to be cast off irrevocably. (Fathers apparently are not so forgiving!)

A late medieval parable makes clear this relation between Christ and Mary:

A certain Brother Leo saw in a vision two ladders, the one red, the other white. On the upper end of the red ladder stood Jesus and on the other stood His holy Mother. The brother saw that some tried to climb the red ladder, but scarcely had they mounted some rungs when they fell back; they tried again but with no better success. Then they were advised to try the white ladder and to their surprise they succeeded, for the Blessed Virgin stretched out her hand and with her aid they reached heaven. *(Quoted in* The Glories of Mary, *by Alphonsus de Liguori, edited by Rev. Eugene Grimm. Redemptorist Fathers)*

Mary—Mediator of Grace

The split between justice and mercy, between Christ and Mary, also allowed the stereotypes of female fickleness and partiality to color the ideas about Mary as the mediator of grace. Mary is sometimes seen as vain and capricious in her favors, in dubious situations protecting those devoted to her. She can be temperamental toward those who neglect her worship, not unlike her secular counterpart, the "lady" of courtly love tradition. Mary's image is modeled after contemporary feudal society. She is the beautiful mistress of the heavenly court, the tender and merciful confidante of the trembling peasant, who could plead his cause with her against the anger of the lords of the castle.

One could be sure that Mary's Son would not refuse any favor asked him by his mother. In this way Mary becomes a humanizing element in an otherwise intolerable opposition of heaven to hell, of divine majesty to human sin. Mary becomes the mediator of all graces, the center of popular piety. Persons dare not hope to find their way to heaven except through her mediation. In the New Testament it is said that only through Christ is there a way to the Father. Now it is added that only through Mary is there a way to Christ.

The idea of Mary's co-redemptive role in part goes back to the early analogy between Christ as the new Adam and Mary (or the church) as the new Eve. As the Fall (Gen., ch.3) came through cooperation between a man and a woman, so redemption must also come through cooperation between a man and a woman. The urge to include Mary in the work of Christ as advocate of sinners and finally as co-redeemer reflects an uneasiness with a doctrine of human salvation mediated by the male alone. If humanity, male and female, is to be redeemed, the female too must play a cooperating role in the work of salvation.

The Immaculate Conception

In the Middle Ages the doctrine of the Immaculate Conception came into its own. The doctrine arose first as a kind of accessory to the doctrine of the virgin birth of Christ. It was felt that only if Mary herself was cleansed of all sin could she provide the properly untainted womb for the birth of the sinless one. As early as Augustine the view arose that she had been preserved from all actual sin. But opinion remained divided throughout the Middle Ages about her preservation from original sin.

In A.D. 1140 the great medieval saint, Bernard of Clairvaux, himself notable for his Marian devotion, objected to the institution of a feast of the Immaculate Conception at Lyons in France. He argued that, at most, one could say that Mary was sanctified in her mother's womb and so preserved from all actual sin. But to argue that she was preserved from original sin would mean that she herself was the product of a virgin birth and not of normal human sexual generation. Here it becomes clear that behind the doctrine of the Immaculate Conception there lies the Augustinian idea that the sexual act itself is debasing and that original sin is transmitted to the child through it.

The great theologians of the thirteenth century, Thomas

Aquinas and John Bonaventura, also rejected the doctrine. For them all humanity is included in the sin of Adam. All persons stand in need of redemption by Christ. If Mary was conceived without sin, then she would be an exception to this universal rule. She herself would not need Christ's redemption. Yet these theologians also believed that she had been sanctified in her mother's womb. The fruits of grace to be won by Christ were applied to her by God in advance. The womb that bore the sinless one must be preserved from all taint of sin.

Here we see a tendency to regard sin as a kind of material "pollution" that is "contagious." The desire to define Mary as free from sin comes from the feeling that to bear the sinless one, one must be free of any contact with this "infection."

In the fourteenth century the distinction between Mary's conception in original sin through sexual generation and her subsequent cleansing in the womb was narrowed by defining the cleansing as coinciding with her conception. In practice, therefore, she was never subject to sin. This cleansing was still the work of Christ's grace. So it could not be said that, by nature, she was removed from the human need for Christ's redemption.

In the eighteenth century, a further distinction was made by theologians between Mary's active conception (by her parents' sexual act) and her passive conception (fertilization and infusion of her soul). By the nature of the first she was conceived in sin. But the results of the sin were prevented from taking effect because the merits to be won by Christ were applied in advance to her. The purpose of this ingenious distinction was to allow it to be said that Mary never was in original sin even from the first moment of her conception. Yet this does not make her an exception to the general rule that all mortal flesh is subject to the penalty of the sin of Adam and must be saved by the grace of Christ. It was in this form that the doctrine of the Immaculate Conception was finally declared a dogma of the Roman Catholic Church by Pope Pius IX in A.D. 1854.

Natural Goodness

The spread of the doctrine of the Immaculate Conception in late medieval theology was closely associated with a school of theology called "nominalism." The nominalists believed that the image of God was still intact in every human being. That image was the basis on which one could independently respond to God's grace. By "doing what is in you," persons may bring their souls to that state of repentance and goodness which God is bound to reward with the gift of divine grace won by Christ's death. This state of natural repentance corresponds to the original goodness of created humanity. The sinner could not win sanctifying grace by natural good works. But the natural will could bring the sinner to that state of repentance and restoration to natural goodness which God is bound to reward with the gift of sanctifying grace. This is quite different from Paul's view of justification by faith alone.

The doctrine of the Immaculate Conception provided this late medieval theology with a model of the original or unfallen state and of the natural goodness of humanity. This natural state is the image of God in every person and is the ground of redeeming grace. Mary, who never lost this state of created goodness, is the representative of "pure nature," the capacity within created nature for perfection. In the language of Catholic piety she is "our tainted nature's solitary boast."

The theological importance to Mariology in this theology of Immaculate Conception, therefore, lies in her "pure" humanity. As the representative of humanity in its original goodness, she becomes the anticipation of its restoration and fulfillment at the end of history. In her will be realized the final glorification of the human community and of creation in the new heaven and the new earth, in cooperation with the redemptive work of God in Christ. Theologically, Mary is the personification of the church, the New Israel, the hope of humankind.

In our next chapter, on the Reformation, we shall see that

Mariology is criticized by the Reformers, not because Mary is a goddess, but because she stands for a more exalted image of humanity than they were willing to accept.

For Thought and Discussion

1. The idea of Mary and/or the saints as mediators expressed a Christian concept of the solidarity of the church as community. Salvation was mediated not just by relation to Christ or God, but by Christians' relationship to one another. The community created a "cloud of witnesses," not only among the living, but even among those of past generations, who are in solidarity with one another in communicating grace. How might we express this idea today?

2. Can persons become something that they don't have a potential to become "from the beginning"? Does the possibility of salvation suggest that creation must have a "potential" to be saved? How could we understand or express this idea that creation has a potential for the goodness that God gives it? Do you find it useful that a woman is the symbol of this capacity of creation for perfection? Why, or why not?

10

MARY AND THE PROTESTANTS

With the Reformation in the sixteenth century, Mariology quickly began to fade among Protestants. Even in the Roman Catholic Church, Mariology was still speculative and did not have dogmatic status. Neither the immaculate conception nor the assumption had been declared dogmas. So the Reformers actually did not make a big issue of devotion to Mary in their criticism of Rome. Martin Luther, especially in his early sermons, even showed a kind of medieval piety for the virgin. He simply affirmed that the true basis of Mary's dignity was as a humble believer who received God's grace. Symbolically, she might have been the first believer, but any special blessings given her were the result of Christ's dignity and not due to her special merits.

Reduction of Marian Devotion

There are three aspects of Protestant thought that were important in reducing Marian devotion. First, there is the Protestant devotion to the Bible. Since stories such as the assumption were not part of the Biblical record, their status is in doubt. Yet the Reformers also recognized that deduction from what is contained in Scripture may be true Biblical teaching. On these grounds both Calvin and Luther accepted the title "Mother of God" for Mary. This title expressed the mingling of the attributes of the human and the divine in the

70

incarnate nature of Christ. Calvin, however, declined to advocate the title because he believed its strict theological meaning was not properly understood by the people.

A second important change made by the Protestant Reformation was the abolition of monasticism. The Reformation rejected virginity as the highest expression of Christian devotion. It also rejected institutionalized celibacy of any kind. The antisexual spirituality that supported celibacy thus began to disappear. Instead, the Reformation identified itself with the patriarchal tradition of the Old Testament and the pastoral letters of the New Testament. The family was made the foundation and model for the religious community or the church. Marriage was no longer seen as inferior to virginity in the Christian life. Sex was no longer viewed as a venial sin even within marriage. The Biblical blessings upon children were restored.

The Christian was no longer seen as someone trying to live "angelically" as in that heavenly age to come where there is no more marrying (Luke 20:35). This state is reserved for heaven. It is not anticipated on earth. The Christian lives in the created world and participates in its processes. Marriage is the normal state for the Christian, for both clergy and laity.

With this reaffirmation of married sexuality, the impulse behind doctrines such as the Immaculate Conception and the Perpetual Virginity of Mary was cut off. Protestants did not immediately reject all these traditions. But Mary's sinless status began to be reevaluated by the Reformers. The way was opened for a later Biblical scholarship to recognize that Mary and Joseph probably lived as a normal married couple after Jesus' birth and that the brothers and sisters of Jesus mentioned in the Gospels were probably indeed siblings and not "cousins."

A Psychological Change

This reaffirmation of the goodness of marriage was also important on the level of psychology. It may not be possible

71

to repress our sexual instincts without that repression reappearing in some other form. People compensate for lack of real sexual relations by creating fantasy love objects. For twelve centuries the theologians and clergy of the Western church had lived as celibates whose sexual feeling could not be expressed honorably with the opposite sex. The beautiful virgin of heaven was then a safe idealization to whom these feelings could be directed. At the same time such devotion reinforced aversion to real women who were thought defiled by sex and procreation.

Mary was the spiritual "mother." Love for her allowed the clergy—monks and theologians—to cultivate a lively devotion to the feminine image and yet to negate women at the same time. But with the conversion of the Reformed clergy to married status, the psychological need for this fantasy disappeared. One could deal with the actual reality of genuine women and not a fantasized idealization.

But the Biblical and the psychological reasons for the fading of Mariology in Protestantism are only part of the story. There is also a theological element in Reformation thought that undercuts Mariology. This third element in Protestantism diminishes the role of the "feminine" as a symbol of the human nature of the church in relation to God. The radical Protestant definition of justification by faith alone redefines human nature in a negative way.

In the Mariology of the Roman Catholic and Eastern Orthodox traditions, there is a concept of the goodness of the created being that links it with the holy being of God. Grace reaffirms the true holiness of natural being, which is itself founded on creative grace. Mary, as a coordinate symbol with Christ, joins together the holiness of created being and the holiness of divine being. In the dogma of Immaculate Conception, Mary is "pure nature," who affirms the capacity of created beings to bear the holiness of divine being.

Any such coordination between nature and grace was abhorrent to the strict theology of the Reformation. The image of God in the human being was believed to be inoperative after the Fall. Nature, here and now, is ruled by sin. God's grace must be seen as totally beyond what are now its "natural" capacities. Humanity stands in a purely passive relation to God's grace. Neither the church nor Mary as its symbol can be seen as a cooperator in the drama of salvation. The feminine, as the symbol of human nature in its receptivity to God, is excluded from visibility. The only actors in view are the Father and his agent, the God-man, Christ.

Women Subordinate

Despite their reaffirmation of the goodness of marriage, the Reformers showed no disposition to elevate the role of women to be representatives of Christ in the preaching and teaching of the church. On the contrary, the teachings of Genesis and of Paul were vigorously reaffirmed to maintain the subordination of women in the church, in the family, and in society. It was assumed that women properly should take on only that subordinate role of a creaturely person reacting to the masculine actors: God, his Son, and his representatives, the clergy.

Protestant theology views the symbols of male and female as divine headship and creaturely subordination. The husband's headship over the wife is like God's Lordship over creatures. This has been restated by Karl Barth in recent times. Barth sees the relationship of male to female as the model for the covenant of God and creation in grace. Therefore he believes the relationship of male to female necessarily partakes of the same "order" as the relationship of God to creatures. This means masculine headship over female obedience. Woman should know that she "loses nothing thereby." Indeed, in this view, she would be rejecting her place in the order of creation and of grace if she rejected this secondary status. She must recognize that, in rank, she is a woman and therefore behind and subordinate to man.

The disappearance of the independent female image in Protestantism is compensated for by a feminization of the image of Christ, especially in Protestant pietism. This feminized Christ may have something to do with the secularization of public power in modern society. The church then becomes confined to the private, domestic sphere of society. The church is taken out of the male roles of power and activity and is relegated to the private, supportive role of the female. It seems to be along these lines that the independent female image disappears in Protestant theology and piety. Christ's human nature appears as feminine (creaturely) but his dominant (divine) identity is masculine. Thus the church's leadership is overwhelmingly masculine.

To be sure, liberal Protestantism, under pressure from secular liberal trends in society, has recently allowed a small number of women into its ordained clergy. Yet the intense tension and discord generated by this new militancy of women in the churches and seminaries and the great reluctance to place ordained women as full pastors of congregations manifest a basic contradiction between a token acceptance of equality and the actual subordination of women that is still a part of Christian theology.

For Thought and Discussion

1. The traditional Catholic image of Mary was very much dictated by a culture that made virginity the highest Christian calling. The changes created by the Reformation had a lot to do with the rejection of this concept of Christian virginity and the exaltation of Christian marriage.

   How does the image of woman change as the culture of the church changes from the idea of virginity to the ideal of marriage?
   Which view do you think is most helpful to the "liberation" of women?
   What do you see as good or what as bad in the exaltation of the virgin ideal?

What do you see as good and what as bad in the exaltation of the married ideal?

2. It is often said that the Christian ideal of Jesus is itself a "feminine" ideal. What do you think is the meaning of this "femininity" of Jesus?

   What effect does this "femininity" of Jesus have on men in the church? What effect on women in the church?

11

MARY
AND PROBLEMS
WITH CONTEMPORARY
CULTURE

In our last two chapters we shall evaluate the meaning and usability of Mariology as a symbol for women. However, a reinterpretation of Biblical symbols may not be enough. We have to think about the whole of the Old and New Testaments and Christian history within the larger development of human consciousness in modern culture. We have to look back over the broad sweep of the history of culture in which a male ruling class conquered nature and the female. Only by understanding what this conquest does to women can we begin to create a new cultural psychology that will enable women to come into their own as fully human persons.

A Clue Among the Goddesses?

Some women studying religion think that women should go back to the goddess figures that preceded the Bible, whose memory Mariology faintly preserves. But the image of the goddess may also be part of the problem rather than part of the solution. The ancient goddess seems stronger and more independent than the image of Mary. But does she not depict an earlier stage of male domination over nature with the woman a symbol of "Nature"? Like Mary holding Jesus, the big goddess from whose lap the god-king of ancient societies reigned seems to stand for an aspect of human culture in which the male still thinks of himself as the child of a big mother. He imagines her as the means by which he becomes king over the universe. He sees himself as her darling and favorite. He uses her to become dominant.

What, then, shall we do about the centuries of cultural thinking that have made ("male") mind dominant over ("female") body, ("male") man over ("female") nature, ("male") God over ("female") creation? It is not enough just to restore to visibility the "female" sides of these relationships and to say that now our religion has given women "their place." As long as we continue to take our symbolism of women from this tradition, women will be forced to represent the passive "underside" of everything.

It is certainly not enough just to change our words and no longer to speak of God as "he" or the church as "she." We must look at the dynamics of this language and at the modes of thought that underlie them. How has our language been shaped by a history of domination so that one side acts like a tyrant and the other side like a subject? How has male domination shaped our whole world view about all relationships into a pattern of super- and sub-ordination? We have to rethink our language on many different levels. This is really the problem of beginning to create a new culture.

God's Power—A New View

How can we think about God in new ways that are not sexist? Should we say that God is female rather than male, or both male and female? Maybe we have to go deeper than this. We have to ask why it is that the symbolic relationship of God to the world has been seen in terms of domination and subjugation and so provides a model for a similar social relationship. Can we think of divine transcendence in another way? God's transcendence could be seen not as a "power over" that reduces creation to a servant status. Rather, it could be seen as the ground and power for created being to exist and to be continually renewed. God is thus both the ground of being and its continual power for aspiration to new being.

God is the End, the Beginning, and the Center of the new being of creation that is ever seeking to become the true image of its divine foundation. God is then the foundation of the unique personhood and the being of every human person, female or male. God is Person, but neither male nor female. Both male and female are made in God's image (Gen. 1:27). God is also one and not two. So the uniqueness of God guarantees the uniqueness of every human self. Every person is called to be a unique person in her or his own right, not just a shadow of someone else.

People are also called to be full human beings as members of community, not as islands unto themselves. In human relationships in community we also have to get rid of the symbolism of dominance of men over women and the dependency of women. This old social situation was the model for the religious symbols of male dominance and female subordination. That model means that only one person is an actor and has the right to be a full person. The other is a servant and nurturer. It is a one-sided relationship. We need instead models for two-sided relationships. Each person must be allowed to be fully human. Each person must become both an "I" and a "Thou" to the other. Each person must become both an actor and a helper of the other.

How Mariology Could Help

Mariology can allow the male to experience himself as "feminine" or to experience what is called his "feminine side." Even the most patriarchal theologian is able to experience himself as the passive, receptive vassal of divine activity and grace, since all people in the church are thought of as "feminine" in relation to the dominant "masculine" ego of "God." This doesn't mean that receptivity is a bad thing. It is a capacity that mature people need to develop in order to enter into relationships. But when only one side, the male, is active, and the other side, the female, is receptive, women never learn to be real people, and men never learn to listen to and help others. Real reciprocity between people is destroyed by this sexist model of male activity and female receptivity. This means that the very possibility of genuine relationship is destroyed.

There can be no real relationship where receptivity is identified with powerlessness, dependence, and self-negation. True receptivity to others is possible only for a person who has some independence and self-esteem. The sexist model of male activity and female receptivity makes relations between men and women into what psychologists call a "sadomasochistic" relationship. This means that one is either domineering, patronizing, and punishing toward subordinates or fawning, servile, and suffering before superiors. Men may experience this latter type of "femininity," but one has to question whether it contributes to healthy relationships.

The split between dominance and receptivity in male psychology has created a demand for the repression of the whole personhood of women as a group. By identifying powerless passivity with "femininity," women are commanded to be the specialists in self-denying and auxiliary types of life. Men then monopolize the feedback of both the male and the female types of life. This means that man, male and female, appears as a person only in the male. Women exist as helpers and reflectors of this process of male self-becoming.

Women must question those men who are quick to say, "But we too must experience our 'feminine' side," as long as femininity is still identified with the passive, auxiliary "side of man." This concept of a "feminine side of men" only reinforces a model of humanity in which women appear as the nurturers and servants of a selfhood that can actively appear only in males. We have to imagine a new psychodynamics of relationship that no longer identifies activity with domination and receptivity with dependency.

The New Model

The model of human relationships that we are looking for is one of "reciprocity." This means that in a healthy relationship each person actualizes himself or herself by the same process through which each also supports the dignity and self-actualization of the other. This calls for a change of roles between men and women in society. This means that they divide roles in a new way that permits reciprocity.

Instead of woman's being the full-time nurturer of children, the homemaker, and the supporter of male activity on the job or in school, we would divide things so that half of the time men play such roles for women and half of the time women play these roles for men, or that they work on jobs together in society and at home. Each is concerned to support the other in his or her self-realization and, in turn, is supported in his or her own aspirations. This will demand more than a change of consciousness or a change of cultural symbolism. It also means a change of power relationships between the sexes. We will have to reorganize the economy and the way jobs are structured and located in relation to the home.

FOR THOUGHT AND DISCUSSION

1. List all the qualities you regard as "feminine" on one sheet of paper. List all the qualities you regard as "masculine" on another. On a third sheet list the qualities you regard as those of a "mature human being."

   Compare the lists. Is the "mature human being" closer to the first list or the second? What is the source of our stereotypes of "masculinity" and "femininity": social organization or nature?

2. How would you envision the creating of reciprocal relations between men and women in daily life? Have differ-

ent members of the group chart what they see as unequal relations, from their own experience. Then get them to develop scenarios for reciprocal relations in these same situations. What changes would be necessary in individuals and in society to change the situation from unequal to reciprocal relations?

12

MARY
AND THE HUMANIZATION
OF THE CHURCH

Is there any model for liberated human relationships in the Gospels? Can we free the symbols of Christ and Mary, or Christ and the church, from being models of male dominance over female passivity? The concept of male dominance still preserves the old order of sin. It does not yet present us with the real meaning of Christ, which is the new order of reciprocal relationships within a humanity reconciled with God. Is it possible, then, to think of the image of Christ and the church in a liberating way where reconciled relations to God are expressed through reconciled relations to one another? As The First Letter of John says: "He who does not love his brother [sister] whom he has seen, cannot love God whom he has not seen. And this commandment we have from him, that he who loves God should love his brother [sister] also." (I John 4:20–21.)

Teachings of Jesus

There are in the Gospels teachings of Jesus that might help us to make a start toward a new understanding of human relationships in society and the church. For example, Jesus solemnly warns his followers not to imitate, in their ideas of church leadership, the religious leaders of their tradition. These people, he says, practice virtue with their lips, but by their conduct are haughty and ostentatious.

82

You are not to be called rabbi, for you have one teacher and you
  are all brothers and sisters.
And call no man father on earth, for you have one Father who
  is in Heaven.
Neither be called masters.
He who is greatest among you shall be your servant.

(Matt. 23:8–11
paraphrased by author)

There are other passages in the Gospels that reflect Jesus'
concern that social relations in the Christian community not
reflect the power relationships of the society of his time:

You know that the rulers of the Gentiles lord it over them, and
their great men exercise authority over them. It shall not be so
among you; but whoever shall be great among you must be your
servant, and whoever would be first among you must be your slave;
even as the Son of Man came not to be served but to serve, and
to give his life as a ransom for many. *(Matt. 20:25–27)*

The Christian church has often used this language of Jesus
about Christians as servants or "ministers." But it has not
often followed the real meaning. It has confused the meaning
of this preaching in two different ways. First, the church has
often set up leaders who were lords and princes. Then it has
tried to baptize this lordship by calling it "service." But the
ministry that is a ministry of service does not seek power for
itself. Rather, it uses power to empower others. It particularly
supports the empowerment of those who have been put
down: women, the poor. Only in this way do people become
equals, and so a community of service becomes a real possibility.
  The second way of confusing the language of servanthood
is complementary to the first. The servitude of women, or
servant groups, or slaves, has been justified in the name of
"Christian service." Through this service those who are low-
est on earth will be highest in heaven. But we should remem-
ber that Jesus called males, especially his male disciples, to

servanthood. He did not recommend this to people who were already slaves. The one person whom he rebukes for being "too much occupied with serving" is a woman, Martha. (See Luke 10:38–42.) Martha was only acting the part of the good Jewish woman of her time when she stayed in the kitchen and called for her sister to return to the kitchen to help her in serving. It was Mary who was out of her place. In the religious tradition of that time, women were not supposed to be disciples of the rabbi or to join the circle of disciples who might have been listening to his teaching.

The rabbis had specifically forbidden women to be taught in the religious circles of disciples. Jesus is really overthrowing this practice in his culture when he affirms Mary's right to come out of the woman's role of servanthood and to join as an equal member in the circle of disciples.

> Mary has chosen the good portion, which shall not be taken away from her. *(Luke 10:42)*

A Community of Equals

In Jesus' culture it would be hard to imagine that he could have called God anything other than Father. But in the way he is using the name of Father in the passage we quoted above (Matt. 23:9), he seems to be trying to establish a different relationship of God to the community. Instead of the concept of God as Father providing a pattern for setting up a group of "fathers" in the church who lord it over the laity, the way husbands lorded over wives in Jesus' society, the God whom Jesus is speaking about is One who creates a community of equals, a community of brothers and sisters.

This suggests a revolution in human relations and in our symbols of God's relationship to society and creation. If God as parent does not create a "hierarchy" of leaders, but rather creates a community of equal persons who live in mutual service to one another, then perhaps we also cannot think of God as that sort of "big leader" who lords it over other people. Our ideas of God have to be changed also into a new understanding of relationship. In the New Testament this change in our images of God is suggested by the teaching that, in Jesus, God has "emptied himself" and become a servant. (See Phil. 2:5–11.) God too refuses to be seen as a lordly "king," but rather is like a servant, who comes down to earth to empower those who have been broken and to create the community of the new creation.

If Christ represents this "emptying out" of God into service, then he too cannot be seen as "lord" in a way that reestablishes the lordship of some people over other people: the lordship of males over females, clergy over laity, princes over subjects, rich over poor, or white over black. Jesus' resurrected being consists of an emptying out of this kind of lordship. Jesus pours the power of the Holy Spirit back into creation, to bring about a community of love. In Christ, the power of traditional "lordship" is called to repentance and conversion. It is called to give up domination and instead to spend itself in service to support and affirm the selfhood, dignity, and goodness of those who have been oppressed, of those who have been made the slaves of its domination. Perhaps it is in this sense that we should understand the tradition that the new humanity, the church, the community of the redeemed, appears, not in the person of the male, but in the person of the female.

Women as the Church

Women as the church represent those subjugated people who have been lifted up by the emptying out of God's power in Jesus. They have been empowered to become conscious and self-actualizing persons. Women represent the church in the same way that Jesus also makes the "poor," the nobodies of the earth, represent the head of that new humanity which will lead the way into the redeemed world.

We are saying something quite different from what Christians have usually understood by the "feminine" nature of the church. We are not saying that such women only represent females. Much less are we saying that they represent what has been called the "feminine" side of masculine properties. Rather, women as the church represent that whole of redeemed humankind which can only be liberated and reconciled when the victims have been empowered to be persons and when power itself has been transformed.

If Christ represents the emptying out of a divine power that puts itself at the service of others, then Mary, or the church, represents liberated humanity. Mary represents the *person of the church* from the perspective of the conversion that has to go on in history, and between people, to overcome dehumanizing power and suppressed personhood. From the perspective of final salvation, the new humanity is neither male nor female, neither slave nor free, neither Jew nor Greek, neither black nor white (see Gal. 3:28).

But we can have this final perspective only in hope. Here and now we are going through a process of change. All of us must become full persons by using the power and privileges we have to affirm the humanity and dignity of those people who have been the historical victims of egoism and power in the ruling classes, races, and sex.

But who is this Mary who represents the church? The Christian tradition made the mother of Jesus, Mary of Nazareth, into the chief representative of the church. She particularly represented the mystery of the incarnation, that is, the mystery of the coming of Christ into the world. But this identification of the church with Jesus' mother tended to put us back into a framework where the one certified historical accomplishment that women were allowed to have was motherhood. It also translated the meaning of Christ's coming into biological language. Rather, it should have recognized that the real meaning of Christ's coming was grace, the freely given gift of God's Word freely heard by the power of the Spirit. Jesus himself rejected a special honor to his mother simply on the grounds of her maternity, when he said to the women who praised the "womb that bore you, and the breasts that you sucked": "Blessed rather are those who hear the word of God and keep it!" (Luke 11:27–28.)

Other Marys

Luke elevates this understanding of Mary as the church by putting her maternity itself in the context of her hearing the Word of God. In the Annunciation story Mary's maternity is taken out of a biological context. Christ comes because she hears and responds to God's Word. (Ch. 1:38.)

Perhaps we should also see that there were originally other "Marys" in the Gospel story who represented this responsiveness to Christ. They have been overshadowed by the symbol of Mary, the mother. These other Marys are not his mother, but his women disciples. They are Mary of Bethany, "who chose the better part," or Mary Magdalene, who did not flee before the show of imperial might, but stood by the cross and sat by the tomb when the other disciples betrayed Jesus and ran away. It was she who was the first to grasp the Easter faith and tell it to the others. By exalting Mary, the mother, we have perhaps deprived that Mary, who was not his mother but his disciple and friend, of her great accomplishment: being the first to understand the resurrection faith that is the foundation of the church. This is that faith in God who

Has scattered the proud in the imagination of their hearts,
. . . has put down the mighty from their thrones,
and exalted those of low degree.

(Ch. 1:51–52)

For Thought and Discussion

1. In this article the meaning of Christian ministry is discussed as the "ministry of service" which does not estab-

lish power over other people but empowers others and creates equality and reciprocal relationships.

Do you think this is the functioning concept of ministry in churches today? Why, or why not?

How would you envision churches' being run and organized that had this concept of ministry?

How is such a concept of leadership different from the concept of leadership found in other social organizations?

2. In this chapter two different concepts of the "femininity" of the church have been discussed: *(a)* the traditional concept of the church as "bride of Christ"; and *(b)* the woman as a representative of "oppressed people," the representative of those who must be affirmed to create a liberated humanity. Discuss these two concepts. Characterize the main elements of each. Do you think that the second concept is a useful change that corrects problems in the first concept or not? What problems seem to arise in the second concept?

Donald M. Stine

FOR THE LEADERS
OF STUDY GROUPS

Using the symbol of Mary, the mother of Jesus, Rosemary Radford Ruether invites us to dialogue on the Bible, the Christian tradition, and the contemporary church. Ruether attempts to raise our consciousness by telling us about Mary from several vantage points. Each point of view makes its own contribution. Like the pieces of a puzzle, it takes all the pieces to make the final picture.

One piece is the role of the ancient goddess in the Near Eastern part of the world where our Bible was born. The Old Testament reacts to Near Eastern culture and provides a number of feminine symbols that relate to the God of the covenant. Consider, for example, Israel as God's bride and the Wisdom of God.

The New Testament is more precise. Here we meet Mary as a real person with human reactions. She has a humble recognition of God's action in and through her. Paul picks up some of the Old Testament symbols and talks about the church as Christ's bride. These symbols are the Biblical bases for the feminine face of the church.

Ruether then turns to aspects of the church's tradition as it developed in the ancient period and during the Middle Ages. This is another piece of the puzzle—Mary in traditional Catholicism with the Protestant reaction to that tradition from an overwhelmingly male point of view.

Finally, Rosemary Ruether does a lot of reflecting on the

Biblical view of Mary in the light of current concerns of women in society and in the church.

Like any complicated puzzle, it takes time and patience to put the parts of this study together. The end result is a picture of the "Feminine Face of the Church."

This study is an invitation to reflect upon and dialogue about Mary—the feminine face of the church.

Options for Organizing the Study

The material in this book can be organized for study in several convenient ways. Each of the twelve chapters addresses a discrete portion of the subject. Therefore each chapter could become the focus of one study session. The plan of this option would simply be to follow the structure of the book.

Part I. Mary in the Bible—six sessions

Part II. Mary in the Church—six sessions

An obvious adaptation of this plan is to have two separate but related courses of six sessions each: Course I—Mary in the Bible, and Course II—Mary in the Church. Groups that are more interested in Bible study may simply focus upon Part I. If this option appeals to you, it is recommended that you also include Chapter 12 in your planning as an appropriate conclusion to your study.

Many groups will be interested in the subject but will find it impractical to commit themselves to a twelve-session venture. The whole book can be covered, admittedly in less depth, in an option of five sessions. The outline of such a plan might look like this:

Mary in the Old Testament (Chapters 1–3)—one session

Mary in the New Testament (Chapters 4–6)—one session

Mary in the Church Tradition (Chapters 7–9)—one session

Mary and the Protestants (Chapter 10)—one session

Mary and the Humanization of Culture
    and the Church (Chapters 11–12)—one session

For groups that meet monthly, it is even possible to do something worthwhile with a three-session option:

Mary in the Bible (Chapters 1–6)—one session

Mary in the Church (Chapters 7–10)—one session

Humanizing Culture and the Church (Chapters 11–12)—one session

The following suggestions for the leader's preparation follow the scheme of the book chapter by chapter. They deal with background understanding of the book's contents including additional resources that might be consulted. They also contain procedures that might be followed in the study group. If your option is to study the material in fewer than twelve sessions, there will be more guidance here than you can possibly use. Whatever your plan for study, it is hoped that you will find some suggestions that you can adapt in a helpful way.

1. Mary and the Ancient Goddess
I Kings, ch. 18; Acts 19:21–41

Objective: *To trace the development of the symbol of the ancient goddess as it bears on the Christian symbol of Mary.*

Preparation of the Leader

1. Read the Introduction to Part I.

—What issues are raised in the Introduction? Jot these down. Refer to them often as the study proceeds.

—Make a list of questions that Chapter 1 raises for you.

2. Answer for yourself the following questions:

—How do you account for the fact that "many Biblical symbols, festivals, and institutions also were common to the ancient Near Eastern cultures"? For example, consider the symbol Messiah and what Ruether says about it. See what you can find out about the background to the Jewish Feast of Passover or the institution of the Temple. An encyclopedia or *The Interpreter's Dictionary of the Bible* may help you.

—How is the ancient goddess a symbol of life? (Consider the woman as birth giver, the birth of the gods in mythology from the "world egg" or womb.)

—How is the goddess both virgin and mother? To whom in particular was she mother? (Note the article "Isis," *The Interpreter's Dictionary of the Bible*, Vol. E–J, page 750.) What are the main features of the "Prayer to Ishtar" (see Chapter 1).

—What further contribution do the Greek myths make to the idea of the goddess? How have these myths and the religions of the Roman Empire (like the Isis cult) influenced Christianity?

Procedure with the Group

Before the first session with the group, ask for volunteers who will make brief five-minute reports on the following subjects: the issues the course may raise (see the Introduction to Part I); several illustrations which show that some Biblical material was borrowed from surrounding cultures; the goddess as a symbol of life; the goddess as virgin and mother (the power behind the throne); the rarefied goddess as virgin; the goddess of the mystery religions (life after death).

In the light of these reports and to conclude the hour, as group exercises use the questions "For Thought and Discussion" that follow the chapter.

2. Mary and Israel—God's Bride
Hosea, chs. 1 to 3; The Song of Solomon

Objective: *To discover the images of the feminine that the Old Testament carries.*

Preparation of the Leader
1. Consider the following main points:

92

—"In the Old Testament there is no divorce between history and nature." (See Isa., ch. 24, as an illustration.)

—"The old language of nature was taken over in the Psalms and the Prophets to express the alienation or reconciliation of Israel with God." (See Amos 4:6–13 and ch. 9:13–15.)

—"The ancient mother goddess was eventually repressed in Hebrew worship. But images associated with her survived in hidden or allegorical ways." (Observe the language of marriage in Hos., chs. 1 to 3, and the language of love in The Song of Solomon.)

2. Do a little research on Hos., chs. 1 to 3, and The Song of Solomon (also known as The Song of Songs). *The Interpreter's Bible*, Vols. VI and V, will help you. The notes in a study Bible like *The Jerusalem Bible* are also an aid.

3. Write out your own answers to discussion questions that accompany the study article.

Procedure with the Group

If your objective is to discover the feminine in the Old Testament, write on the chalkboard the following points: "The ancient mother goddess was eventually repressed in Hebrew worship. But images associated with her survived in hidden or allegorical ways."

Divide the group into two subgroups.

Assign to one the study of Hos., chs. 1 to 3. Have it investigate the statement: "The relationship between God and Israel is like a marriage between a husband and a wife."

Assign to the other group one or two poems of The Song of Solomon. Choose from ch. 1:5 to 2:7; ch. 2:8 to 3:5; ch. 3:6 to 5:1; ch. 5:2 to 6:3; ch. 6:4 to 8:4. The prologue is ch. 1:1–4 and the conclusion is ch. 8:5–7a with some appendixes, ch. 8:7b–14. Have this group discover the language of love—emotional, warm, passionate, alluring—and notice the language of nature—the world of flowers, trees, and animals.

Have the two groups share findings with each other.

3. Mary—The Wisdom of God
Proverbs, ch. 8

Objective: *To investigate in the Wisdom Literature another root of the feminine face of God.*

Preparation of the Leader
1. Understand the chapter. The following sequence of ideas may be of help:

GOD'S FEMININE SIDE

The Old Testament Materials:

God's Wisdom
See Prov., ch. 8, and the apocryphal Wisd. of Sol. 7:22 to 8:4.

God's Presence with Israel
See Ex. 40:34–38 and Num. 9:15–23.

God's Spouse—Israel
See Hos., ch. 2.

Jewish Thought:

The Exile
Separation of Israel, God's spouse, from God. God's presence remains with a separated Israel.

The Present Time
The sexual union of husbands and wives—a sacramental expression of the future reunion of God and Israel.

The Future
Completion of the marriage union between God and Israel.

2. Study the Biblical materials that relate to the theme of the feminine side of God.
—Prov., ch. 8, and the apocryphal Wisd. of Sol., 7:22 to 8:4
—Ex. 40:34–38 and Num. 9:15–23
—Review Hos., ch. 2.

3. Reflect upon the questions for thought and discussion that accompany the chapter.

Procedure with the Group
Prior to the meeting of the study group assign each of the following topics to two or three persons: (1) God's Wisdom—What It Means, from Prov., ch. 8, and the Wisd. of Sol. 7:22 to 8:4; (2) God's Presence with Israel —Its Description, in Ex. 40:34–38 and Num. 9:15–23.

Have each small group of two or three persons present its findings.

To conclude, have full group discussion on the questions for thought and discussion that accompany the chapter.

4. Mary—Mother of Jesus
Luke 1:26 to 2:20; Matthew 1:18 to 2:23

Objective: *To pinpoint in the New Testament the roots of the church's traditional teaching about Mary.*

Preparation of the Leader
1. Survey the following passages in the New Testament in which feminine symbolism is prominent: Gal. 4:4; Eph. 5: 21–33; Rev., ch. 12. What views of the woman emerge in these passages? How do these views enlighten our understanding of Christ and of his church?
2. Focus on Matt. 1:18 to 2:23 and on Luke 1:26 to 2:20. Prepare as follows:
—Compare and contrast the two passages. See if you can determine the essential differences in the two accounts.
—What role does Mary play in relation to Joseph in the Matthew account?
—How would you characterize Mary's self-understanding in Luke's account?
—How do you evaluate what Rosemary Ruether says to conclude about the Luke passage: "It is from the Lucan tradi-

tion within the New Testament that we have the fountain-head of Mariology"?

3. Study carefully what Rosemary Ruether says about the virgin birth. How have you understood this teaching? What new insights are provided here?

4. Ponder the thought and discussion materials for this chapter.

Procedure with the Group

Have a panel discussion on Luke 1:26 to 2:20 emphasizing Mary as central actor in the drama of salvation described here. Have the panel consider the following points: (1) Mary as an active participant in the drama of Jesus' birth; (2) Mary as "an independent agent cooperating with God in the redemption of humanity"; (3) the expression of God's purpose for humankind in her song, the Magnificat (ch. 1:46–55).

As there is time, have the group reflect on the meaning of the virgin birth.

5. Mary and the Mission of Jesus
Mark 3:31–35; Matthew 12:46–50; Luke 8:19–21; John 2:1–11; 19:25–27

Objective: *To reflect upon the tensions between Jesus and his family as another aspect of the New Testament view of Mary.*

Preparation of the Leader

1. Study Mark 3:31–35; Matt. 12:46–50; Luke 8:19–21.
—What differences do you observe among the three texts?
—Look into the context of Luke 8:19–21. What does it mean to "hear the word of God and do it"? (V. 21.)
—What do all three passages imply about Jesus' relationship to his mother and family?

2. From the chapter find other evidence from the Synoptic Gospels that points up Jesus' negative relationship with his family. At what point does that relationship change?

3. Study John 2:1–11 and ch. 19:25–27. How does Rosemary Ruether interpret these materials? Do you agree or disagree? Why?

4. How does the chapter view Mary Magdalene? What do you think?

5. Give attention to the questions in "For Thought and Discussion" following this chapter.

Procedure with the Group

Divide your study group into two subgroups. Provide pencil and paper. Be sure each member has a Bible.

Have one group study Mark 3:31–35; Matt. 12:46–50; Luke 8:18–21; 12:49–53; 11:27–28. Have each person write an essay on: How is the relationship between Jesus and his family characterized? Allow about half an hour.

Have each person in the other group write a brief reflection on the relationship between Jesus and Mary Magdalene as an unconventional woman. (Note John 20:11–18.)

Share essays.

6. Mary and the Femininity of God
Ephesians 5:21–33

Objective: *To sum up the feminine symbols of the Biblical tradition.*

Preparation of the Leader

1. One mark of good teaching is to pull together the principal ideas being studied. In short, review . . . review . . . review! The opening two paragraphs of the chapter help this process.

2. Don't expect what is discussed to be strictly logical. Biblical language is highly emotional, that is, *symbolic.* (If the word is not clear, look up "symbol" in an unabridged dictionary.) The church, for example, may be thought of as bride, mother, and "virginal mother."

3. Two of the three points of the chapter may be tied

to Biblical materials. They are:

—"Mother Church, Bride of Christ": Eph. 5:21–33; Rev. 12:1–6; see also ch. 21:1–4.

—"The Virgin Soul as Bride of Christ": an allegorical or mystical interpretation of The Song of Solomon. (For some background on its allegorical interpretation, see the article "Song of Songs" in *The Interpreter's Dictionary of the Bible,* Vol. R–Z, pages 422–423.)

4. Sum up for yourself the main points of Part I of the book, "Mary in the Bible."

5. Try the exercises under "For Thought and Discussion." Decide whether you want these to be group exercises.

Procedure with the Group

Have three different persons prepared to report on each of the three main points of the chapter (10 minutes each):

Mother Church, Bride of Christ

Wisdom: The Femininity of God

The Virgin Soul as Bride of Christ

Have a Bible study (30 minutes):

1. Read Eph. 5:21–33 aloud.
2. Ask the following questions:
    a. How is the husband-wife relationship symbolic of Christ's relationship to the church? Illustrate.
    b. How does Christ's relationship to the church transform the husband-wife relationship?

The Layman's Bible Commentary, Vol. 22, by Archibald M. Hunter, will help.

7. Mary—New Eve and Perpetual Virgin

Objective: *To come to understand the origins of the church tradition about Mary as new Eve and perpetual virgin.*

Preparation of the Leader

1. Your task in this part of the course is to build on the

Biblical materials that have been discussed in Part I. The objectives for the second are twofold:

To understand the traditional teaching about Mary as it developed in the early, medieval, and modern periods of church history.

To ask what this tradition might mean to us today—as Christians, as participants in contemporary culture and in the church.

2. Review the Biblical materials that provide the symbolism of Eve and Mary the virgin.

—Gen. 2:18 to 3:24. (If you were a member of the ancient church, how would you describe a new Eve who would contrast with the old Eve?) (Paul introduces the idea of the new Adam [Christ] who contrasts with the old Adam. Observe the contrasts in Rom. 5:12–21.)

—Look again at Matt., ch. 1, and Luke 1:26–56 for references to Mary, the virgin. What does the context say in each case? Note particularly v. 38.

3. In the *Encyclopaedia Britannica* or other reference work, look up "Gnosticism" and "Asceticism." What view of the person is involved? For early gnostic-ascetic teaching rejected by the apostle Paul, see Col. 2:20–23. For a sample of letters by Ambrose and Jerome in which asceticism is made the ideal, see "Letter 63" of Ambrose (pp. 274–276) and "Letter 108" of Jerome (pp. 362–369) in The Library of Christian Classics, Vol. V, *Early Latin Theology,* translated and edited by S. L. Greenslade (The Westminster Press, 1956). If you are near a university or a seminary library, you may find the complete text of "The Protevangelium of James" in *The Ante-Nicene Fathers,* Vol. 8, edited by Alexander Roberts and James Donaldson (Wm. B. Eerdmans Publishing Co., 1951), pp. 361–367.

Procedure with the Group

1. Draw attention to the topics to be covered in Part II.

2. Have a panel discussion on the pros and cons of the ascetic way of life. Have the members of the panel prepare

themselves by reading the chapter carefully and by investigating the meaning of "asceticism." Reference might be made to Col. 2:20–23.

3. Have the full group consider how this ascetic view of the person influenced the developing tradition about Mary as the new Eve and perpetual virgin.

4. Conclude the hour by considering No. 2 under "For Thought and Discussion" following Chapter 7.

8. Mary—God's Mother!

Objective: *To consider together both the theological and the human reasons for the transfiguration of Mary.*

Preparation of the Leader

1. For perspective on what you are studying, read again the Introduction to Part II of this book. For the last session you investigated Mary as the new Eve and as perpetual virgin. For this session you are looking into the teaching about Mary as "Mother of God" and the doctrine of her assumption.

2. Think again about the background to the developing tradition about Mary.

—Refer again to Chapter 1.

—How is the Mary of popular religion a Mary of the agricultural world (like the ancient goddesses of fertility, an earth mother)?

3. Ruether then carries the mother symbolism one step farther: "Mary as Mother of God."

—State in your own words the contrasting points of view in the theological controversy as to whether it was right to speak of Mary as "Mother of God."

—How did popular piety understand this? What do the following words in the chapter mean to you: "It is the birthing of the divine power through which the world itself was created"?

4. What does the "Assumption of Mary" mean? For background, look at the brief articles in *The Interpreter's Dictio-*

nary of the Bible, Vol. A-D, "Assumption of the Virgin," and Vol. K-Q, "Moses, Assumption of." Compare the Biblical traditions of Enoch (Gen. 5:24) and Moses (Jude 9).

5. Give some attention to the "For Thought and Discussion" questions (at the conclusion of the chapter) on divine power and the resurrection.

Procedure with the Group

1. Write on the chalkboard: *Two key factors in religion are the concepts of power and of the afterlife.*

Ask: In our everyday Christian life, what is power? What are some emotionally satisfying words or expressions (Biblical or otherwise) that describe divine power? Have the group share. How did the person of Mary have attached to her the attributes of power? (The symbol of the Gospel of Bartholomew is *fire.*)

In our everyday Christian faith, how do we think about the afterlife? Have the group share more imaginative language. Refer, for example, to I Cor., ch. 15, or to Rev., ch. 21, for the Biblical language. Share with the group the meaning of the medieval church's teaching on Mary's assumption.

2. To conclude, ask: What difference does it make to you whether divine power and the afterlife are put in feminine rather than masculine terms? Discuss the implications of both.

9. Mary—Grace and Goodness

Objective: *To sum up the dual role of Mary in the medieval view.*

Preparation of the Leader

1. Here we have come to the final two features of the medieval development of the church's view of Mary: Mary as mediator of grace and the immaculate conception.

2. Review what was said earlier about Mary as new Eve and as perpetual virgin (Chapter 7).

3. Ponder the two views of Mary that are presented in the chapter:

—How Mary represents humankind before God in Christ (mediator of grace). (Compare and contrast this point of view with I Tim. 2:5–6.)

—How Mary represents God to humankind (the immaculate conception). (Compare and contrast what the chapter says about this with Rom. 5:12–21.) What view of the human being does each point of view represent?

Procedure with the Group

1. Write the following words on the chalkboard:
mother
human being
salvation

2. Have the group associate freely on each word. That is, what images of mother come to mind? (Think, for example, of the mothers portrayed on television.) What is the group's basic view of the human being? (Good, evil, weak, strong, disruptive, reconciling, etc.) What is the group's view of salvation? (Delivering human beings from evil or fusing the good inherent in human beings with God who is good.)

3. Make a list of contrasts under each word on the chalkboard.

4. In the medieval point of view, how does Mary play the good-mother role? (Refer to the story of Brother Leo in Chapter 9.) Help the group to see two sides of that good-mother role:

Mary represents humankind before God (mediator of grace). Thus Mary's work parallels Christ's and feminizes it. (Have someone read I Tim. 2:5–6 aloud to the class.)

Mary represents the divine spark of God to humankind (the immaculate conception). (This is another view of how God and humans get together.) (By way of contrast, have Rom. 5:12–21 read aloud.)

10. Mary and the Protestants

Objective: *To debate the traditional view of the feminine face of the church among Protestants.*

Preparation of the Leader

1. Reflect on the medieval teaching about Mary:
—On a feeling level how did you react to this teaching?
—If you reacted negatively, what reasons can you think of for your reaction?

2. Now read the chapter carefully. Observe that Protestants rejected Marian doctrine on four levels:
—The Biblical. (Certain doctrines such as the Assumption were rejected as non-Biblical.)
—The social. (The Reformation rejected monasticism and reaffirmed marriage and family.)
—The psychological. (Genuine sexual relationships in marriage obliterated the need for a fantasy devotion to Mary.)
—The theological. ("The feminine, as the symbol of human nature in its receptivity to God, is excluded from visibility.")

Procedure with the Group

1. Form two teams and debate the proposition: *Since the Reformation, Protestants have maintained the subordination of women to men.*

2. In preparing the teams and introducing the subject, consider these points:

The Reformation was a reaction against Roman Catholic doctrine. Marian doctrine was rejected on a number of grounds. (Are they valid or not?)

Some Biblical texts imply the subordination of women. (Can you find some that do? others that don't?) Protestants affirm the Bible.

Yet the feminine has come into the church in a new way. (What do you think of Rosemary Ruether's insistence: "The disappearance of the independent female image in Protestantism is compensated for by a feminization of the image of Christ"?)

3. Encourage full group response to the debate.

11. Mary and Problems with Contemporary Culture

Objective: *To begin to do some solid reflecting on the implications of this study on Mary for human relationships.*

Preparation of the Leader

1. Delineate the issue that the author is discussing in this chapter. Consider the following question: "What then shall we do about the centuries of cultural thinking that have made ('male') mind dominant over ('female') body, ('male') man over ('female') nature, ('male') God over ('female') creation?"
—Test the validity of this thinking in your own experience.
—Find illustrations.

2. What alternatives does the author propose to the domination model in human relationships?
—What view of God does this imply?
  What Biblical metaphors help you here? See Deut. 33:27 (God as support); Jer. 3:4 (God as friend); Job 19:25 (God as redeemer or vindicator); Phil. 2:5–11 (Jesus emptied himself).
—What do you think the relationships between men and women ought to be in order for reciprocity to take place? How does the Bible help you here? See Gal. 3:23–28. (How has the language of domination been transformed here? In the light of what Rosemary Ruether says, ponder ch. 5: 13–15.)

Procedure with the Group

1. Write the main issue of the chapter on the chalkboard.
2. Have the group share illustrations, pro and con, of the main issue.

104

3. Divide the group into two subgroups. Have each discuss one of the following points. Have one person report to the full group:

A view of God that deemphasizes domination.

A view of human relationships that stresses reciprocity. (The Biblical references in No. 2 under "Preparation of the Leader" may help.)

4. To conclude, ask: What practical implications (for church, community, family, single relationships, etc.) do you draw from all of this?

12. Mary and the Humanization of the Church

Objective: *To explore possible ways in which the church may be humanized.*

Preparation of the Leader

1. What theme is carried over from the preceding chapter? Study the Biblical passages involved.

2. Analyze the notion of "servant"—in the home, in public places such as restaurants, in "public servant," and in the church's image of "the missionary," "the minister." What does the author say is the Christian meaning of "servant"? What Biblical passages corroborate this?

3. Read the story of Mary and Martha (Luke 10:38–42). Do you agree with the author's interpretation? What difference would it make in the life of the church if we took the story seriously?

4. What do you think of the author's insistence that the feminine nature of the church (symbolized by Mary) is pictured as the image of a subjugated people set free? Think of some ways in which this idea might be put into practice.

Procedure with the Group

1. Divide into subgroups. Provide pencil and paper. Ask each subgroup to investigate the following Biblical passages

to discover the kind of servant the church needs:

    Matt. 23:8–12

    Matt. 20:25–27

    Luke 10:38–42

Have each person write his or her own brief descriptive statement of the new image of the servant.

2. Come back together. Share statements. Think together as to how the church might be humanized with the Biblical idea of the servant. Be specific. Don't neglect the symbol of Mary, which in the author's view carries the possibility of humanizing the church. Consider exactly what Rosemary Ruether means by this. Give the whole group a chance to react.